SLAYING NEW YORK

Curated by Leigh M. Clark

Aurora Corialis Publishing

Pittsburgh, PA

OTHER COLLECTIVES BY LEIGH M. CLARK

Slaying Southwest Florida

Slaying Tampa Bay

Slaying Atlanta

Slaying Nashville

Slaying Sarasota

Slaying Chicago

Slaying Boston

Slaying Vegas

Slaying Naples

Slaying Orlando

The Dream is in Your Hands

The Dream is in Your Hands: She Can Do It

Living Kindly: Bold Conversations About the Power of
Kindness

Table of Contents

A Note from Slaying Series Author Lori-Ann Marchese

New York has been the heartbeat of my journey—from Bravo TV to red carpets, magazine features, and years of media work that shaped the woman I am today. Being featured in multiple Slay the USA series books is an honor that reflects my commitment to strength, resilience, and elevating women everywhere.

Standing beside the powerful women in this book—women of courage, grit, and unstoppable spirit—reminds me why New York is so special. This city built my confidence, sharpened my ambition, and continues to inspire me to rise higher.

Slaying New York is not just a project.
It's a sisterhood.
A celebration of power.
And a reminder that we rise stronger—together.

Introduction
Leigh M. Clark

This one's extra special.

As the curator of the Slay the USA series—someone who's interviewed thousands of women across the country and published more than two hundred fifty authors—each city holds its own place in my heart. But there is no city that has had a bigger impact on shaping me than New York.

I was born in 1979, right at the edge of the '80s, to parents who hailed from two very different corners of Nassau County—my mom's side rooted in the quiet, wooded luxury of Cove Neck on the Long Island Sound, and my dad's side grounded in the working-class heartbeat of Hicksville, the same hometown where Billy Joel went to high school with my dad. That blend of saltwater serenity and pure New York grit shaped the rhythm of my childhood. We were multi-generational, fiercely loyal, loud in all the ways that matter, and unmistakably New Yorkers through and through.

Some of my earliest memories were built on the Sound. Christmas mornings began with brunch at my grandparents' house—cousins flying in from California, aunts and uncles squeezed into every room, and layered conversations that blended into joyful chaos. Back then, family felt enormous and permanent.

But childhood doesn't stay untouched for long.

When I was seven, we moved to Setauket, in the Three Villages. It became the place I would claim as home for most of my life. I lived right across from my elementary school and walked there every morning, believing life was predictable and gentle.

Then life shifted again.

By third grade, cancer took my dad's father. By fourth grade, it took my mom's father too. Two patriarchs gone in two years.

Holidays changed. Rooms felt emptier. The Sound looked the same, but everything felt different.

And yet, in the grief, the women in my family rose.

My mom's mother discovered independence—redecorating, dreaming again, reclaiming her life. My dad's mother traveled the entire world after her husband passed. These were the first women I ever saw reinvent themselves. The first women I ever saw slay.

The grief had not ended yet, however. In 1992, at one of my brother's football games, my mom's mother mentioned a lump. Within months, she was gone too. Three grandparents lost before middle school. My one remaining grandmother—and the family who circled around her—became my anchor, my grounding force back to everything New York truly meant to me.

Despite the grief, I was stepping into the middle-school era with a growing sense of identity. I had finally climbed the social ladder: friends with mega-houses, weekends spent riding jet skis on the Sound and hanging out in downtown Port Jefferson, afternoons in kitchens larger than the homes I grew up in. I landed a part in *West Side Story*—the blonde Mexican (a very time-stamped casting choice)—and I was convinced eighth grade would be my best year yet.

And then, right in the middle of all that teenage ascension, my parents told me we were moving to Chicago.

I was in the middle of a school year, I had finally landed the cool friend group, and I was right at the height of my pre-high school glow-up. I thought my life was finally taking shape—and then suddenly, I was packing my entire world into boxes.

In a moment of pure fourteen-year-old desperation, I begged my parents to let me stay in New York and live in my friend Nora's pool house so I could finish out the year. I made solemn vows about visiting them for holidays and being mature enough to handle it. Needless to say, that didn't fly.

I did, however, get to go on a trip with her later that summer.

When we arrived in Illinois, I wasn't eased in gently. I was thrust straight into high school in the middle of the school year—a brand-new building, brand-new hallways, brand-new social dynamics, and absolutely no familiarity. And because I was a New Yorker, blending in wasn't an option. The way I talked, the speed I moved, the energy I carried... I stood out whether I wanted to or not. New Yorkers don't blend—we announce ourselves simply by existing.

But I grew from that, too.

My parents let me go to Ireland with Nora that summer, and between Chicago, Ireland, and New York, my accent softened into what I now proudly call non-regional diction—though if you get me talking about bagels, coffee, or Times Square traffic, the New Yorker comes right back out.

By twenty, the gravitational pull of New York was too strong to ignore. I'd worked in restaurants, skipped my original plan for journalism school in Arizona, and knew I needed to return home. I enrolled at NYIT in the early 2000s—around the Kelly Clarkson era of American Idol—and earned my bachelor's degree in advertising.

I joined the world's smallest but fiercest sorority, Sigma Iota Sigma. We weren't many, but we were mighty. Those women became lifelong friends; even now, as mothers, we still take trips together. New York gives you friendships that don't fade—they deepen.

After graduation, I moved back to Chicago briefly to explore my next step. I opened my first marketing business and landed six clients quickly—but something in me knew I wasn't fully ready. So I packed up my car, grabbed the thousand dollars I had left, and drove back to New York.

My goal?

Work on Madison Avenue within a month.

And I did.

In my twenties, I thought forty-five thousand dollars in NYC was a fortune. I couldn't even afford to live there—I could barely afford my train pass. I commuted two hours each way from all the way out near the Hamptons, paying nearly four hundred dollars a month for the train, walking around Manhattan in jeans that fit exactly right and shoes that made me feel important. The glamor wore off quickly, but the grit stayed.

Within months, a recruiter in Melville told me he believed I was meant to be a significant earner—not in advertising, but in sales. He connected me to ADP, and my trajectory shifted instantly.

I spent years building my life and career in New York—at twenty-eight, I was a director of marketing of a prominent software company—that is until 2008 hit. The recession devastated the city and the country beyond it. I lost my job, and then my heat, then my water, and finally my internet and cable. I sat in that cold apartment watching *The Secret* on DVD on repeat, trying to manifest a way forward.

Eventually, I packed up everything—my belongings, my pride, my dreams—and moved to South Carolina to rebuild. Shout out to my parents for hosting my "Failure to Launch" party for the year they housed me. I climbed back from sushi waitress to manager in Mount Pleasant, S.C. before I was ready to get back to the rat race. Living in the south made me want to slow down a bit. I soon found myself in Florida working for ADP again, realizing I had more inside me than corporate sales... though it would take years before I acted on it.

But even in Florida, New York never left me.

When I launched Kindleigh in 2012, my nonprofit and kindness movement, I made New York a focal point. I paid off strangers' layaways at Macy's. I covered holiday purchases in Times Square. I handed out gifts to people experiencing homelessness on Christmas. Whenever I wanted to do something that mattered, I returned to New York. That city is where impact always felt the most real.

Eventually, by 2015—still running the charity and feeling purposeful—I simultaneously landed my dream job in marketing at Salesforce. Because I was so undeniably a New Yorker, they let me live in Florida while keeping all my clients, accounts, and territory in New York. My home was in Florida, but my office was steps from Bryant Park in NYC—I reveled in the imagery hosting nonprofit leadership summits at the top of the Salesforce building with expansive 360 degree views from Brooklyn to New Jersey out the windows behind me. I was back.

I flew back constantly and not just to work, to see my grandmother, my sorority sisters, my family, my roots. I did so many acts of kindness, as there were opportunities everywhere I looked throughout the city.

Even when I didn't live there, New York lived in me.

And when the Slay the USA series officially launched in 2023, I always knew New York would be one of the crown jewels of this movement. I just needed to wait until I had truly become the woman who could honor the women of this city.

Because this edition is filled with women who represent the very soul of New York. Women who've had quantum leaps in their careers and in their lives.

A scrappy chef who clawed her way from back kitchens to Michelin honors and the Food Network.

Women who not only slayed on Bravo, but left their mark on New York Fashion Week, the Grammys, and more.

A woman who earned both an Emmy and an Edward R. Murrow Award.

A woman who has traveled to one hundred twelve countries and counting.

Another who worked her way from food service all the way up to becoming an internationally acclaimed travel photographer.

And so many more—women whose grit, tenacity, ambition, resilience, and heart embody everything this city stands for.

And while I've lived in many places—making "Where are you from?" surprisingly complicated—my answer always circles back to the same truth:

New York is my origin story. My foundation. My touchstone.

Bringing my son, Carter, and my partner, Twain—the love of my life—to New York recently was one of the most meaningful experiences of my lifetime. It was the first time either of them had ever been to NYC, and watching them look up at Times Square in total wonder, wandering through Chinatown, riding through Central Park, and standing outside Madison Square Garden with all the iconic New York energy swirling around us felt like sharing a piece of myself with them — the part of me shaped entirely by this city.

Because New York is iconic.

And this book is about icons.

Women who rise.

Women who slay.

Women who make their mark on a city that makes no promises and takes no nonsense.

This isn't just another chapter.

This isn't just another book.

This is my love letter to New York—the city that always slays.

Compassionate Storyteller. Truth Seeker. Good Human.

Virginia Huie

I'm a journalist, so I won't bury the lead. Never stop chasing your dreams. My journey to becoming a television reporter was filled with naysayers. I heard a lot of, "No, you can't do that," and, "You'll never make it."

I believed in me and my dreams.

For me, it's making a difference through storytelling. When I get to do that, there's truly nothing that feels better. Nothing!

I grew up surrounded by stories of perseverance. My father was fourteen when he emigrated from China to the United States. My mother, also from China, came when she was sixteen. When they immigrated to America, they didn't have much. My father's side of the family owned a small laundry business in

Manhattan. My grandparents ironed and folded shirts, and hand-wrapped them in brown paper. My mother's side of the family owned a Chinese restaurant in Virginia where they cooked take-out meals seven days a week. My father was the first in his family to graduate from college. He became an electrical engineer. My mother, a self-taught seamstress, worked in a bridal shop. I grew up watching them work so aggressively hard in pursuit of the American Dream. Their example of the immigrant hustle planted the seeds of my strong work ethic that served me well throughout my life.

As a child growing up on Long Island, I never thought that I would be on TV, let alone reporting in New York. I was a quiet and shy kid. English was not my first language. I learned to speak English in nursery school. In college, I majored in economics to prepare for a career in finance.

The turning point came when I got an internship at a bank. Right away, I realized it was not for me. So, I asked myself, "What am I passionate about?" "What am I good at?" I'm a good writer and good listener, and I'm curious about people, places, and things. So, I set my sights on becoming a journalist.

Breaking into television reporting was extremely tough; *no* was the soundtrack of my job search. I received so many rejection letters that I had enough to fill three binders. I saved those letters because I believed every *no* was just a little step closer to that *yes*, if I kept pushing. I remember one news director told me, "Maybe you should try a different line of work." But I didn't give up. When I was offered a job as an associate producer in Washington, D.C. I took it. It gave me the opportunity to keep learning and build my resume tape. Within a year, I received a job offer to be an on-air reporter in Des Moines, Iowa. I took the leap from the East Coast to the Midwest, and I never looked back.

After two years of reporting on farming, extreme weather, and education at KCCI-TV, I jumped fifty-four markets to Seattle, Wash. I returned to New York to report at News 12 Long Island shortly before September 11th. I currently work at Newsday TV.

My assignments have taken me to places I have never been, from the halls of Congress and the White House to jail cells and naval warships. As a journalist, I've had a front row seat to historical moments the public isn't typically privy to—and wow, I've met some amazing people along the way. Presidents, professional athletes, war heroes, and more.

The most gratifying moments for me are the ones where I've been able to use my storytelling to share someone's story that wouldn't have been told otherwise. Like the story of Isaiah Bird, a homeless six-year-old wrestler who was born without legs. My report lifted Isaiah from obscurity to the national spotlight. Viewers inspired by Isaiah's can-do spirit organized fundraisers for him. A generous donor gave Isaiah and his family an apartment. ESPN produced a documentary. Nike featured Isaiah in a commercial with Colin Kaepernick.

Covering 9/11 and the War on Terror also impacted me profoundly as a journalist, especially when talking to people who lost loved ones. I've learned so much about strength of character from people as they were going through the worst thing that's ever happened to them. Every story reminds me it's a privilege to listen, to learn, and to tell.

Looking back at my journey, I'm grateful for every opportunity and experience. Every challenge and obstacle made me stronger. If you have a dream, chase it at all costs. The people saying *no* aren't living your life. Listen to the whispers in your heart. When you follow your heart and work hard, amazing doors open.

About Virginia

Virginia Huie is a multiple Emmy Award-winning and Edward R. Murrow-honored journalist whose compassionate storytelling has made a mark in broadcast reporting across New York.

Formerly a longtime reporter at News 12 Long Island, she earned acclaim for covering human interest stories with authenticity, especially those of veterans and Gold Star families.

Now a reporter and fill-in anchor at Newsday TV, she brings a rare blend of news acumen, empathy, and narrative skill. Her reporting doesn't just inform; it invites viewers to see the world with both honesty and heart.

Winner of seventeen Emmy Awards and five Edward R. Murrow Awards and recipient of more than one hundred thirty Emmy nominations, Virginia also has been honored with two New York Festival International Gold Medal Awards for "Last Letters Home" and "Faces of Ground Zero," a Deadline Club Award for Feature Reporting for "Fighting Spirit," two New York Associated Press Broadcasters Awards for General Excellence of Individual Reporting and several New York Press Club Awards. Virginia also won a Gracie Allen Award and a national Gabriel Award for her Holocaust love story, "Girl With The Apple."

Born in Manhattan, Virginia grew up on Long Island. Prior to her work at News 12 Long Island and Newsday, Virginia was a reporter at KCCI-TV in Des Moines, Iowa, and KSTW-TV in Seattle, Wash. She began her broadcasting career as a Leo Beranek News Reporting Fellow at WCVB-TV in Boston.

Virginia graduated *magna cum laude* from Barnard College/Columbia University with a degree in economics and earned a master of arts degree in communication from Stanford University. She is a member of the National Honor Society, Phi Beta Kappa.

A published writer, Virginia's articles have appeared in the *Sacramento Bee*, *The Salinas Californian*, *Boston Globe*, *The Progressive Magazine*, *Newsday*, and college textbooks. She serves as secretary on the board of the New York chapter of the National Academy of Television Arts and Sciences.

Instagram: @virginiahuietv
Facebook: https://www.facebook.com/huie12/

The Art of Becoming

Karen Asprea

I catch myself laughing out loud as I stand inside one of the most magnificent estates I've ever been in—one that I designed—holding a coffee in one hand and one of Michael Jordan's sneakers in the other. The room glows with late-morning sunlight, its glass cases lined with priceless pieces of sports history. The irony isn't lost on me. I've never paid attention to sports in my entire life, and yet here I am, carefully handling one of basketball's most sacred relics. I take a sip, glance at the slightly dirty, game-worn sneaker, and gently place it into its custom glass case, thinking to myself: how did that little girl from Brooklyn who used to sketch faces in her notebook margins end up here?

I never set out to be an entrepreneur. I just followed curiosity, beauty, and a fascination with how people feel in the spaces they live in. Looking back now, design wasn't a career choice—it was a language I was born speaking.

I grew up in Brooklyn in the eighties and nineties, surrounded by the noise and pulse of a big Italian immigrant family. There was always food cooking, the tube TV blasting news on RAI, and at least three conversations happening at once. My mother, my grandmother, and the women in my family were strong, stylish, and emotionally intelligent. They ran the household, the family, and, in many ways, the world around them. They also had an effortless sense of glamour—the perfume, the jewelry, the way they set a table. Without realizing it, they were teaching me my first lessons in design: how atmosphere shapes emotion, and how beauty can be a form of care.

As a child, I was obsessed with faces. I drew constantly, trying to capture what people felt more than what they looked like. My parents noticed my artistic streak early, and to their credit, they never discouraged it, even though "artist" wasn't exactly a stable career path for an Italian-American family that had worked so hard to make it. They just wanted me to be happy.

By high school, I was the girl who could draw—the one who saw the world in light and shadow. I attended Leon M. Goldstein High School for the Arts and Sciences, and later Pratt Institute, which felt like stepping into a dream. My time at Pratt expanded my world, but studying at its sister campus in Copenhagen changed my mind forever.

Copenhagen taught me that design begins with function, not form—that beauty is a byproduct of purpose. I lived in a city where every chair, window latch, and sidewalk was designed to enhance daily life. The Danes build from nature outward, using wood, stone, and light. I learned that simple materials, used thoughtfully, can create profound emotional impact. That lesson never left me.

After college, I chased adventure and followed a handsome man to his family estate in Vienna, where I landed an internship at an architecture firm. I was in my twenties, trying to use AutoCAD in German and living off espresso and cigarettes. It was demanding and exhilarating, but it taught me discipline—how to show up, be creative across cultures, and deliver no matter how tired I was.

When I returned to New York, I joined a firm led by Costas Kondylis, a renowned Greek architect whose clients were the giants of real estate development: Extell, Related, and the Carlyle Group. I was in my mid-twenties, sitting in rooms where billion-dollar projects were being imagined. I learned more in those years than any classroom could teach me—how the city is built from the inside out, how power moves quietly, and how good design solves human problems elegantly.

Then the 2008 economic collapse hit. Overnight, the firm shrank from hundreds of people to a handful. Yet from the rubble, something remarkable emerged. A few of us rebuilt. I was barely twenty-five, suddenly managing teams and learning to lead not through authority, but through intuition.

Over the next decade, I became a partner in an affiliate firm that I co-founded, leading a team of thirty and designing for some of the biggest names in New York real estate. From watching massive foundation pours to shaping interiors for skyline-defining towers, I poured myself into the work. But even as I thrived, something inside me began whispering for more—not more in scale or fame, but in depth. I wanted intimacy. I wanted meaning.

Then my body intervened.

Out of nowhere, I became very ill. One of my kidneys failed, and I underwent a massive reconstructive surgery that forced me to stop—really stop—for the first time in my adult life. When you're used to running at a hundred miles per hour, being forced to lie still changes you. That recovery was humbling and clarifying. I had to rebuild myself—not just physically, but emotionally. And in that rebuilding, I found my new path.

I decided to start my own firm, a place where design wasn't just about luxury, but about transformation. I wanted to create environments that helped people become who they were meant to be. That's how Asprea Studio was born—first in Tribeca, then expanding into South Florida.

In those early years, my phone began ringing with unexpected calls—from developers, builders, and vendors asking me to design their personal homes. That's when I realized something essential: Trust is the true currency of success. People never forget how you make them feel.

Over the last seven years, my work has taken me into the most intimate spaces of people's lives—not just their homes, but their transitions. I've designed for clients moving through marriages, divorces, births, deaths, career changes, and rebirths. These are moments of chaos and vulnerability, when identity shifts and people crave stability. That's where design becomes sacred.

When someone lets you into their home during those moments, they're not hiring a decorator; they're inviting you into their story. My job is to translate that story into space. My first question is never "What do you want your home to look like?" but "How do you want to feel?" From there, everything unfolds.

I've worked for people whose names you'd recognize instantly, and others who move quietly but shape the world in profound ways. Many of my projects are private, never published, because discretion is part of the trust my clients place in me. Truthfully, I've come to love that quiet. The real beauty happens in those unseen moments—when a client walks into their finished home and tears up because it feels like them again.

There's an art to holding people's stories, especially when they're in the middle of a life-altering transition. I've learned to balance empathy with strength, creativity with structure. One day I might design a legacy home for a family welcoming a new baby; the next, a serene sanctuary for someone whose time is limited by illness. Life and loss, joy and reinvention—sometimes all in the same afternoon. It's taught me that beauty isn't only in what we see; it's in what we feel safe enough to experience.

Design, for me, is emotional architecture. Every line, texture, and source of light carries energy. It can make you feel grounded, inspired, sensual, or strong. The spaces I create are meant to be lived in, not just photographed. I call them "occupiable art"—environments that breathe and evolve with the people inside them.

Being a woman in this industry has had its challenges. Real estate and architecture are still heavily male-dominated, and early in my career, I was often the youngest person—and the only woman—in the room. But I learned something crucial: people respond to presence. You don't have to shout to be heard; you just have to stand firmly in your truth. I stopped trying to prove I belonged and started acting like I did.

Now, when I look around my studio, I see a team of incredible designers who share that same passion for meaningful work. I see a business that grew not from strategy decks or investors, but from word of mouth, trust, and genuine connection. And I see a woman who has lived many lives in one—daughter, artist, partner, patient, boss, builder, dreamer.

Standing in that magnificent estate, coffee in hand, placing those sneakers just so, I realized something: my story isn't really about design, or even success. It's about becoming. It's about understanding that the same instincts that helped me arrange a family dinner table as a little girl—to make it feel warm, intentional, beautiful—are the same instincts that now guide me as I help people create homes that heal and inspire them.

If there's one thing I've learned, it's that transformation—whether personal or spatial—is never tidy. It's messy, emotional, deeply human. But when you approach it with love, awareness, and curiosity, it becomes something extraordinary.

Every home I design tells a story of becoming—and so does mine.

About Karen

Karen Asprea is a celebrated interior designer and founder of the acclaimed New York City-based design firm Asprea Studio. Since founding the studio in 2018, she has established herself as a leader in luxury interior design, specializing in bespoke designs for residential towers, commercial spaces, hospitality projects, and private residences.

Born and raised in Brooklyn, Karen built a distinguished foundation early in her career. After graduating from Pratt Institute, she began working with renowned architect Costas Kondylis, gaining hands-on experience in both commercial and residential design and development in New York. She later joined one of the largest architecture firms in the city, where she co-founded the interior design division—becoming the youngest managing partner in the firm. Karen's background in both the business and creative facets of design inspired her to found Asprea Studio, driving her vision to unite design excellence, elite-level service, and fiscal responsibility.

Asprea Studio is an internationally recognized design firm with offices in New York and Miami, known for interiors that balance enduring elegance with innovative functionality. Under Karen's direction, the studio brings a timeless yet contemporary sensibility to every project, rooted in expert craftsmanship, refined tonal palettes, and the thoughtful use of natural materials.

Karen's work has been featured in leading design publications, including *Architectural Digest*, *The New York Times*, and *Mansion Global*. Her work is widely recognized for its architectural approach and meticulous attention to detail.

Karen divides her time between her homes in New York and Miami.

Instagram: @karenaspreastudio
www.aspreastudio.com

Superstar Isabella Barrett: The Making of a Teenage Mogul

Isabella Barrett

I remember growing up in a whirlwind of glitter, lights, and ambition. I'm Isabella Barrett, and if someone had told "little Bella" that at five years old I would be the star of *Toddlers & Tiaras* and one day run my own fashion label, launch two successful brands, show eleven seasons at New York Fashion Week, and become a millionaire before reaching my teens, I probably would have nodded, smiled, and walked away.

My life has never been typical. I always had a lot of energy, and lucky for me, my older sister decided to do a pageant one weekend and took me with her. I instantly fell in love with the stage, the fact I got to put on little performances and dance. I was all in!

Early Life and Pageant Beginnings

From the very beginning, I was drawn to fashion. My journey started in the pageant world, where I quickly found myself thriving. I was crowned Little Miss America in 2012, and by the time I was around ten years old, I had earned more than fifty crowns and over eighty titles.

But for me, it was never just about the tiaras. I genuinely loved performing—creating a moment, owning the stage, and feeling the energy of an audience. That rush stayed with me long after I outgrew the sparkly pageant dresses.

My breakout moment came unexpectedly during a press tour for TLC. I appeared on the *New York Live Morning Show*, and in true Isabella fashion, I just kept talking—excited, animated, and definitely not shy—about my brand and everything I loved. That spark led to more opportunities: becoming a Health Fit Kid for *The Dr. Oz Show*, making cameos on Disney's *Fan La La*, appearing on stage at the MTV Music Awards, and more.

I didn't realize it at the time, but I had taken my fifteen minutes of fame and transformed it into something bigger—I made myself a brand. Suddenly, people knew my name. And with that visibility came opportunity—something I would soon learn to turn into business.

Becoming a Millionaire (At a Very Young Age)

One of the most unbelievable parts of my story is how early everything shifted from pageants to entrepreneurship. While other kids were learning multiplication, I was learning the basics of business.

My first major venture was Glitzy Girl, a jewelry line tailored to pageant girls, dancers, cheerleaders—basically the world I grew up in. With the help of my mom, Susanna Paliotta, we created products that weren't just cute; they were meaningful to the community I understood better than anyone.

By the time I was six, I had already earned my first million dollars. Sometimes I look back and think about how surreal that is. I was a little girl selling jewelry and making business decisions before I really knew what the word *entrepreneur* meant. But I loved it. I loved being part of the process, designing pieces, and watching people respond to something I created.

In 2016, I sold Glitzy Girl. It wasn't an ending, but rather a beginning. I took what I earned and reinvested it into new ideas, new dreams, and bigger goals.

Building My Business Empire

As I grew older, business became more than a hobby. It became my identity, my motivation, and my passion.

One of my proudest creations is House of Barretti, a fashion label I launched because I saw a gap in the market.

- As a teen attending events, walking red carpets, and doing press, I realized something: nobody was designing formal suits for young adults—especially for teens who wanted to look polished, confident, and age-appropriate.
- House of Barretti filled that gap. What started as a suit brand quickly expanded into a full line of fashion, including couture looks, swimwear, hair products, and eventually skincare.

In 2020, I launched a teen-focused skincare line after years of struggling with products that either didn't work or weren't designed for young skin. I wanted to give teenagers something real—clean formulas that made sense for our lifestyle and needs.

That same year, I appeared as myself—a young entrepreneur—on the Amazon Prime reality show Next Big Thing. It was one more step in solidifying my path not just as a TV personality, but as a business powerhouse.

Fame, Work Ethic, and Money Lessons

People often see the glamorous side of my life—fashion shows, magazine features, luxurious trips—and think that's the whole story. But behind every glossy picture, there's work. Real work. By my mid-teens, I had already launched five companies. Some were successful, and others taught me lessons the hard way. Not everything you create is going to shine. That's entrepreneurship.

I've learned about financial responsibility in a way most young people don't experience. One of the biggest lessons? The number on a check isn't the number that actually hits your account. Taxes, expenses, payroll—those things matter. I'm very aware of the difference between revenue and profit, and that has shaped how I invest, spend, and grow.

Of course, I let myself enjoy my success—jet skis, four-wheelers, travel, sneakers. But even then, I see those things as motivation. I create, I work hard, and I allow myself to enjoy the rewards.

Fashion Shows and Public Image

One of the most unforgettable experiences of my career has been putting on fashion shows. With House of Barretti, I've showcased collections during New York Fashion Week, sharing the runway with models who bring my designs to life.

I'll never forget the first time I hosted a VIP after-party for one of my shows. I personally wrote an eighty-five-thousand-dollar check to make it happen. That moment wasn't about the money—it was a statement. I wasn't just the face of a brand. I was the creator, the decision-maker, the one who believed so strongly in my vision that I was willing to invest in it.

Being both a designer and a public figure gives me a unique view of fashion. I understand how clothes feel on stage, how they move, how they make a person feel. And as someone who grew up in front of cameras, I know how important confidence is.

Challenges and Realities

But let's be real—it hasn't all been easy.

Growing up in the public eye means growing up under a microscope. People have opinions about everything—how I dress, how I talk, how I run my businesses. I've faced negativity online, especially because I wear makeup or carry myself with confidence.

I've learned that people who judge don't always see the full picture. They see the photos and headlines, but not:

- The all-nighters.
- The stress.
- The disappointment when a launch doesn't go as planned.
- The pressure of making decisions at an age when most kids are just deciding what sport to play.

Being a young millionaire doesn't erase problems. It just gives you a different set of them. But I am grateful. I know who I am, and I know where I'm going.

Giving Advice and Looking Ahead

If there's one thing I want other young people to take from my story, it's this:

You don't have to wait to be "old enough" to start building something meaningful. You can start now—with whatever you have, wherever you are. I started with a love for sparkles and a TV camera. That foundation became a network, a business, and eventually an empire.

I'm currently writing a book, *A Teen's Guide to Business*, where I share everything I've learned—mistakes included. I want to be a voice that encourages young entrepreneurs to take risks, trust their instincts, and dream big.

My vision for the future is even bigger than what I've already done. I want House of Barretti to become a global name associated with empowerment, creativity, and youth-driven innovation. I want to continue expanding into skincare, cosmetics, and lifestyle products. And I want to keep inspiring others to build their own paths.

About Isabella

Isabella "Bella" Barrett is an American entrepreneur, model, and former child reality star, with ties to Rhode Island and New York. She first gained national recognition through her starring role on the TLC show *Toddlers & Tiaras*, showcasing her early passion for pageantry and performance. She went on to star in many child entrepreneurial shows such as *Getty Made Global*, *Teen Shark Tank*, and Amazon Prime's *Next Big Thing NYC*.

At a remarkably young age, Isabella leveraged her pageant success into business. By six years old, she had already become a millionaire, thanks to her thriving jewelry line, Glitzy Girl, which she co-founded with her mother, Susanna.

Over the years, she continued to build her brand, launching House of Barretti, a fashion label focused on couture suits and casual wear for teens and young adults.

Isabella isn't just a business prodigy—she's also creative. She has released music alongside fellow child star Eden Wood, and her entrepreneurial ambitions have grown to include a teen skincare line aimed at meeting the beauty needs of her own generation. Her bold, driven mindset has made her a role model for young entrepreneurs, and her influence continues to expand.

Despite her high-profile lifestyle, she and her mother have navigated the challenges of early fame thoughtfully: giving back to her favorite charities. Today, Isabella Barrett remains a powerful testament to ambition, innovation, and the entrepreneurial spirit—all before even reaching her twenties.

Instagram: @Isabellabarrett123
TikTok: isabellabarrettofficial
Facebook: Isabellabarrett
www.houseofbarretti.com

A Different Kind of New York Tough

Stephanie Bordas

The sky glowed pink as the sun set over Radio City Music Hall. I was standing on that famous marquee, walkie-talkie in hand, waiting for the director to cue the Rockettes for a *Christmas Spectacular* promo. As a native New Yorker, former dancer, and musical theater lover, it felt like a dream.

Suddenly, my walkie-talkie blared, bringing me back to reality. The NYPD was threatening to shut us down for holding up the traffic. The camera crane was having technical difficulties. The Rockettes were about to go into overtime. We had snow machines ready, but the gorgeous sunset wasn't believable with the special effects. All of this came under the category of "producer problems." It was on me to rejigger schedules, negotiate with talent agents, number-crunch the budget, absorb the director's anxiety, and soothe our nervous clients... among other things. The stress was real. And so was the satisfaction when the cameras finally rolled and the Rockettes made their entrance.

This was the world I'd chosen. It was high pressure, unpredictable, exhausting, and something I was very good at.

Being a New Yorker isn't just a fact of birth—it's a mindset. New Yorkers have grit. We put up with a lot, and expect a lot from our city. Growing up in Brooklyn, I learned early that the city doesn't slow down for anyone, and neither did I. I wore my New York identity like armor, believing that the harder I worked, the more valuable I was, a mindset that served me well in my twenties and thirties. But what I didn't know yet was that relentless momentum can feel like flying right up until the moment you realize you're falling.

My start in production was pure accident. Fresh out of college, I landed a two-week freelance job as a director's assistant—packing gear, fetching coffee, working brutal hours. I didn't love it, and figured that once the job ended, I'd move on to something else.

That gig happened to fall on September 10 and 11, 2001. We were filming at Jones Beach when the city shut down. With cell phones useless, we huddled around car radios for news. The devastation of that day changed everything.

The next morning, I made my way back to the city. The subways were silent. Smoke still rose in the distance, and the air carried a smell I'll never forget. In that moment, I stopped questioning whether production was the "right" career. The work gave me focus, and a way to move forward. So when another call came, I said yes.

And I was glad I did. I climbed the ranks quickly, eventually traveling the world, working with celebrities, and orchestrating massive projects. I thrived on the ever-changing challenges and excitement, and even met my husband on set. But in my heart of hearts, another career path called to me.

I was gifted a point-and-shoot film camera for graduation, and I carried it everywhere. My favorite thing to do was pick up my film from the lab, seeing for the first time what I had created, and gifting the prints to others. Producing, while exciting, meant executing someone else's vision. Photography, on the other hand, allowed me to create my own.

But how does one start a photography business without photographing weddings or newborn portraits? At the time, it seemed like these were the only options, so for years, photography remained a hobby—taking night classes, experimenting with self-portraits, and continuing to snap photos of my adventures around NYC.

Then a friend told me about a boudoir shoot she'd booked as a Christmas gift for her husband. I was curious and signed up for a shoot of my own. While I could see the potential for something amazing, my experience was underwhelming: overdone hair and makeup, plastic heels and feather boas, predictable poses. It felt more like a cosplay performance than anything authentically *me*. But something clicked. *This* was a genre of photography I could get behind, and I knew I could create an environment that was different—a place where women could connect with themselves and walk away with images for themselves that are modern, classic, cool, and very New York.

A spark ignited. I found a mentor, studied the art of boudoir photography nonstop, and began practicing this new style with friends as my models.

My first "official" client was a friend of a friend—a woman in her early forties who'd never done anything like this before. She arrived nervous, apologizing for herself before she'd even taken off her coat.

I handed her a silk robe as we got to know each other. She was a chef, a mother, and recently divorced. I asked her what she loved the most about herself, a question most women struggle to answer, and she was no different. Yet as we talked, her shoulders dropped. She laughed. And when she stepped in front of the camera, I could see something in her shift.

There was no performance, no trying. Just her—powerful, present, perfectly imperfect. I didn't have much technical photography knowledge yet, but I was able to focus on the woman in front of the lens, ensuring she felt comfortable and taken care of, and crafting a strong connection that led to powerful portraits and a style I would eventually call my own.

When she saw her portraits, she cried, saying, "I can't believe that's me." That's when I realized this wasn't just about taking pretty pictures. This was about giving women permission to see themselves as they actually are: beautiful, worthy, enough. Not when they lose ten pounds or get their lips done, or achieve some other arbitrary goal. Right now. Exactly as they are.

Brooklyn Boudoir became real that day.

As Brooklyn Boudoir grew, I was simultaneously climbing the production ladder, landing a job as an executive producer. This meant more money, more steady work, but also more meetings, more desk time, and less creating. I was straddling two worlds, trying to excel in both. Pregnant for the second time, I would wake before five a.m. to answer emails, run between production meetings and photoshoots, squeeze in school pickups and doctors' appointments, and stay up late editing. I told myself I was fine—in fact I was *proud* to be able to balance it all and felt lucky to have two careers I loved. And yet, the more I hustled, the less rewarding both careers began to feel.

One day, shortly after my second daughter was born, while a boudoir client was in hair and makeup at a hotel shoot, I excused myself to pump—which was true, but also a cover for dialing into a last-minute production call. Sitting in that bathroom with a breast pump strapped on, a phone to my ear, and my photography client waiting down the hall, I realized: in trying to be tough and do it all, I was actually failing everyone. Especially myself.

I knew Brooklyn Boudoir would never grow if I kept treating it like plan B. The fears were loud—could I really walk away from production and support my family on photography alone? But my resolve to go for it was louder, and in my heart, I knew it was what I was meant to do.

I gave myself six months to go all in on photography. I taught myself how to run a business, got a studio, made everything official, and then the pandemic hit.

Overnight, all photoshoots were cancelled. I took one last production job during that time. While grateful for the safety net, it also only confirmed what I already knew: my heart was no longer in the film business, and no paycheck was worth the stress or the time away from my family.

What I really missed during the pandemic wasn't the income—it was my clients. I loved showing women their own strength and brilliance, and this was a time when we all *really* needed that boost. Brooklyn Boudoir wasn't just my work— it was my purpose.

Every day, women walk through my studio door carrying the weight of New York—the hustle, the ambition, the high prices, the impossible juggling act. The lawyer between court appearances. The mother finally doing something just for herself. The entrepreneur building something from nothing. These women don't need me to make them beautiful—they already are. What they do need is permission to stop performing, stop producing, stop optimizing. To exist without apologizing. When they step in front of the camera, something shifts. They start to see themselves the way I see them: worthy of celebration. As layers of clothing come off, so do layers of their self-doubt. They remember who they are inside, before the demands of work, kids, and life weighed them down. And they always walk out with a little extra spring in their step, standing a few inches taller than they did before.

One night while editing, my daughter looked over my shoulder at a client's photo—an outtake I'd flagged to delete because it was technically imperfect. "Wow, beautiful," she said, matter-of-factly. The woman was mid-laugh, eyes half closed, the image slightly blurry because I was laughing along with her. My daughter didn't see flaws—she saw someone fully present, joyful, and real. My daughters are watching what I value, what I celebrate, what I call beautiful. And I'm proud I can show them that showing up courageously and imperfectly for yourself, without needing a reason, is what matters.

I'm no longer the woman on that marquee fixing everyone else's problems while my own dreams waited in the wings. Just because I *could* juggle two demanding careers doesn't mean I should have for so long. Just because I *could* absorb the stress, handle the chaos, keep up with it all, doesn't mean that life was serving me.

New York is tough, and so am I. But my toughness isn't about endurance anymore—it's about intention. It's choosing a life that honors who I am, not just what I can handle. It's teaching my daughters—and showing every woman who walks through my studio door—that you don't need permission to take up space, to be seen, to choose yourself, and to have a little fun.

Brooklyn Boudoir isn't just what I do. It's proof that you can walk away from what's depleting you and build something that brings you alive. It's a place where enough isn't something you earn; it's something you already are. That's the New York I choose to live in. And that's exactly what I've built.

About Stephanie

Stephanie Bordas is a Brooklyn-born photographer, business mentor, and educator who transforms lives through the lens and teaches others to do the same. After discovering boudoir photography in 2011, she made the bold decision to leave a successful career as a TV and film producer to pursue her true passion. With no prior business experience, she taught herself both photography and entrepreneurship, launching Brooklyn Boudoir from her New York City apartment.

Through Brooklyn Boudoir, Stephanie has built a reputation for creating luxurious client experiences and editorial-inspired portraits that celebrate individuality, femininity, and self-expression. Her work has been featured in *Rangefinder Magazine* and exhibited at the Smith Theatre, and she has been a guest on The Portrait System podcast, among others.

In 2024, Stephanie launched an educational platform to guide photographers and creative entrepreneurs ready to elevate their craft and grow intentional businesses. Through destination retreats, comprehensive courses, and one-on-one mentorships, she teaches creatives how to stand out in saturated markets, deliver transformative experiences, and build businesses that reflect their values and support their lives.

Known for her supportive, encouraging approach, Stephanie creates spaces where women feel seen, inspired, and capable of exceeding their own expectations. Whether photographing a client or mentoring a fellow entrepreneur, her mission remains constant: helping women see themselves through fresh eyes and step into their power.

As a mother of two, Stephanie understands the importance of building a business that supports your life—one that is profitable, sustainable, and deeply fulfilling.

Instagram: @brooklynboudoir
www.brooklynboudoir.com
www.stephaniebordas.com

Trust Me, It Will Come

Laura Bray

    As I gazed out the airplane window, something felt distinctly different this time. It was a view I'd witnessed countless times throughout my adolescence—that iconic skyline slowly coming into focus, buildings stretching upward like dreams waiting to be realized. Yet I felt butterflies stirring deep within me. Not the nervous butterflies you feel before speaking in front of the student body or the excitement of seeing your high school crush. These were different—profoundly unsettling and strangely exhilarating. I couldn't help but wonder, *We haven't even landed yet; why am I already anxious about leaving?*

I grew up in a loving, supportive household filled with strong, independent women who each played a crucial role in shaping my early years. My driven, entrepreneurial mom was a constant source of inspiration, always showing me what true determination and ambition looked like. My witty, adventurous aunt taught me to embrace life's excitement, always pushing me to step outside my comfort zone. My sweet, nurturing grandmother provided endless warmth and comfort, becoming the gentle heart at the center of my childhood. Someone was always there for cheerleading practices, drama classes, recitals, sleepovers, birthday parties, evenings at the skating rink—if there was an event, I was there, fully supported and thoroughly spoiled as an only child.

Yet, despite this incredible foundation, there was always an underlying feeling of not belonging, of somehow falling short or being out of place. It wasn't something I could pinpoint then, and it would take years before I'd begin to understand it fully.

My twenties were spent serving others, first in the bustling restaurant industry and later practicing cosmetology throughout my home state of Florida. While both experiences brought their own rewards, there was always a lingering feeling of dissatisfaction. It wasn't until I was twenty-eight that I vividly remembered those butterflies from the airplane window ten years earlier. That memory triggered something deep inside me—a realization I couldn't ignore any longer. I needed to leave. I needed something more. I belonged somewhere else. And for me, that place was unmistakably New York City.

With my family's unwavering support, I finally took the leap, moving to the greatest city on earth. The lights, the purposeful strides of passersby, and the intoxicating energy I'd long dreamed of finally became my reality. At twenty-nine, I landed a position at a restaurant I adored, envisioning a promising future filled with opportunities for growth and success. They even entrusted me with running their social media, allowing me to turn my passion for photography into more than just a hobby.

Capturing vibrant images of dishes as they left the expo line, sharing them online to attract eager clients—it felt like the entire world was unfolding before me, full of potential and excitement. But life had other plans. Health challenges, combined with the global upheaval caused by COVID, dramatically altered my path and shifted the trajectory of my dreams.

Living through COVID in Manhattan felt surreal, like a scene plucked from a dystopian movie. The streets of a city that famously never sleeps became eerily silent, broken only by the urgent wails of ambulances. Each evening at precisely seven p.m., we climbed onto our fire escapes, banging pots and pans in solidarity with the brave first responders. Our only genuine connections were maintained through phone calls and social media, as isolation became the unsettling new norm. At the time, my mind coped remarkably well, compartmentalizing the trauma and allowing me to navigate those uncertain days. However, the profound lessons and introspection I gained during this period became powerful catalysts, shaping the next chapter of my journey.

By 2022, I had established myself as a social media manager for over ten Manhattan restaurants. I had pivoted within the same industry, now leveraging digital marketing to help businesses stay afloat in the new post-pandemic landscape. It was exhilarating work, and I found myself channeling my mother's entrepreneurial spirit, confidently hosting events for prestigious brands, connecting influential creators with hospitality groups, producing viral content, consulting on social strategy, and significantly honing my photography skills. My achievements even led me to photograph global celebrities for renowned brands like the Empire State Building and Food Network.

Yet despite my rising success and professional growth, that familiar feeling of unfulfillment began to resurface. Helping other businesses recover post-COVID was incredibly rewarding, yet I found myself yearning for deeper, personal connections. I craved immersion in new cultures, exploration of unfamiliar places, and the enriching experiences of travel.

This realization prompted me to make another bold leap of faith. I decided to leave behind everything I'd built to pursue my true passion—travel and storytelling.

Travel is one of life's most rewarding journeys. It unlocks our deepest courage, dismantles barriers, and reveals the world's unimaginable beauty. Travel fosters genuine human connections, creates unforgettable memories, inspires immense personal growth, and profoundly changes our lives. It's sure changed mine. Over the past couple of years, I've been fortunate to embark on extraordinary adventures, sharing authentic local experiences through social media, blogs, and partnerships with some of the world's most prestigious brands. Nothing fulfills me more than experiencing new destinations and sharing these meaningful journeys with my audience, bringing the world closer and inspiring others to pursue their travel dreams. Making all travel more accessible for curious wanderers is my true passion. I want people to continue to look to me for the most unique, exciting, and enriching ways to explore our beautiful world. Travel is for you, it's for everyone. Whether your dream is hiking Machu Picchu, snorkeling the coral reefs of French Polynesia, festival hopping in Macao, or a romantic kiss under the glistening Eiffel Tower—I finally found my expertise in bringing you the best ways to experience your dreams.

This story is dedicated to all the little girls who are loved yet still feel out of place, to the young women searching for meaning in their twenties, and to those still finding their place in their thirties. It is also especially dedicated to my mother, whose tenacity, patience, and support have been my guiding light all these years. Remember, never stop chasing your dreams. They may arrive when you least expect them—even if you're nearing forty. Some days, I have to pinch myself. Some days, imposter syndrome takes over. But one thing is for sure: We live in a world brimming with possibilities. Believe in yourself, pursue what lights your soul, and know that the feeling of fulfillment is worth every effort and every moment of waiting. You deserve it all.

About Laura

Laura Bray is a dynamic and passionate travel creator, photographer, drone pilot, and entrepreneur behind @lauragramnyc. Her journey into content creation and storytelling began in 2022, driven by a deep desire to reconnect with people, places, and the stories that make travel genuinely meaningful for us all.

Since then, Laura has produced captivating, cinematic, and viral content that bridges luxury hotels, global brands, premium travel experiences, and vibrant destinations with her rapidly growing and loyal audience of over six hundred twenty thousand discerning travelers. Her content consistently reaches millions of viewers, effectively connecting brands with their ideal clientele.

Laura is a passionate advocate for responsible travel, committed to supporting local communities, honoring cultural traditions, and emphasizing preservation. Her mission is clear: to share authentic, impactful stories that resonate deeply, inspiring modern travelers who rely on her uniquely cultivated expertise for trusted recommendations on the most enriching ways to explore the world.

Instagram: @lauragramnyc
TikTok: @lauraexploresitall
linktr.ee/Lauragramnyc

From Hawai'i to NYC

Tanya De Costa

I'm Tanya De Costa, and I was born and raised in Hawai'i (between Wahiawa, Oahu, and all over the Big Island), surrounded by the ocean, land, Hula, music, rituals, respect, and the kind of community that truly embodies the Aloha Spirit. My story, though, begins generations before me with my great-grandmother on my father's side, who journeyed from Puerto Rico to Maui to work in the pineapple fields and sugarcane plantations. She came seeking opportunity, carrying little more than hope, resilience, and the dream of a better life. Her courage laid the foundation for everything that followed.

That strength, mirrored by my grandmother on my mother's side, emulates one of the most independent women I know to date. She grew up with horses and taught me how to care for them, paddled the Moloka'i Channel, powered by pure grit and determination, showing me that women can conquer any current when they trust their own rhythm and collectively contribute. Her spirit taught me that independence and grace can seamlessly coexist, that you can be both fierce and kind, both grounded and liberated.

As one of thirteen kids in my *'ohana (family)*, I grew up in a home filled with beautiful chaos, laughter, competition, humility, and love. As a middle child, my role was clear to me: I was the peacemaker, the negotiator, and oftentimes the glue that held my *'ohana* together. My mom raised us on her own, and her boundless love and resilience shaped how I understood the world. She showed us that showing up, even in hard times, is a quiet kind of strength. When I was twelve, my brothers took me in and raised me, teaching me values that have guided every chapter of my life: to work hard, to move with intention and integrity, and to believe that my imagination is my only limitation.

Those early lessons from my great-grandmother's courage, my grandmother's independence, my mother's openhearted resilience, and guidance from both of my brothers shaped the soul that I am today. They taught me that family isn't just about blood; it's about the people who pour belief into you when you need it most. It's about the *'ohana* you're born into and the one you build along the way from coast to coast.

When I began my career in marketing and global hospitality, I carried all of those lessons with me. I was drawn to the way experiences can transcend borders, how one act of care, one experience, one shared moment can make people feel seen and connected. The most essential human truth is that people want to feel like they belong. Over the past decade, I've led marketing strategies for global lifestyle, entertainment, fashion, spirits, and hospitality brands, driving growth and launching creative campaigns that move people through storytelling, and make the viewer feel something. But more than the milestones or metrics, what's mattered most has been the human connection, the feeling of *aloha* (compassion) that lives at the center of everything I do.

That same sense of connection inspired me to co-found LITO creative, a space born from the belief that culture is what connects us all. At LITO, we're creators and connectors that come from an abundant state of mind, weaving narratives, sparking conversations, and creating a shared sense of purpose through art, music, fashion, and culture. We believe the most powerful stories are often untold, and our mission is to bring light to the obscure, uncovering hidden gems and illuminating others throughout marketing. LITO is an extension of my heritage and my purpose: to honor where I come from while shaping the future with intention. LITO creative is a strategic and bespoke marketing agency that helps global brands and scaling businesses connect with audiences through innovative campaigns, content, experiential activations, and entertainment. We serve as a modern, tactical marketing team that adapts and pivots with poise, delivering seamless, culturally-driven solutions while navigating new media trends.

Beyond my work with LITO, I've come to believe that we're meant to be multifaceted and to pursue our professional paths backed by purpose, not just for achievement but for meaning. That belief inspired me to create Kalena Kai, which is a combination of my brother's name with mine, and loosely translates in Hawaiian to "Pure Ocean." Kalena Kai is more than a sustainable fashion brand; it's a reflection of my *ikigai* (reason for being)—the space where what I love, what I'm skilled at, what the world needs, and what can sustain me converge. Every piece we create weaves together culture, creativity, and consciousness. Each garment is thoughtfully crafted in New York through Atelier Amelia, led by Zhu Ru, a remarkable woman from Hawai'i whose dedication to quality and care mirrors the values that shaped me.

Kalena Kai is my way of staying connected to my roots, a love letter to Hawai'i, a tribute to the ocean that inspires and calms me, and a reminder that sustainability begins with honoring where we come from.

Today, I carry my Hawaiian and Puerto Rican heritage, my family's resilience, and the lessons of my upbringing into every part of my life. I've learned that true success isn't measured by status or recognition; it's measured by connection, creativity, courage, and the impact we leave on others. The woman I am today leads with heart and intention, guided by generations before me and inspired by the stories still waiting to be told.

I am my great-grandmother's legacy, my grandmother's determination, my mother's strength, and my brothers' belief in me. I am a mosaic of love, light, and *aloha*, and my journey is proof that when we follow our purposeful pursuit, imagination becomes the bridge to what's truly possible.

About Tanya

Tanya De Costa is the founder and creative director of LITO creative, a purpose-driven boutique marketing agency based in Brooklyn and built on the belief that *the most powerful stories are meant to be illuminated, shining Light In The Obscure.* At LITO, Tanya and her team are creators and connectors, weaving narratives, sparking conversations, and creating a shared sense of purpose through storytelling that transcends industries. LITO showcases art, music, fashion, and culture in every campaign and partnership, bringing light to the obscure, uncovering hidden talent, and illuminating others through authentic creative expression, while offering marketing solutions for global brands and scaling businesses.

After more than a decade leading marketing for some of the world's most iconic hospitality and lifestyle brands, Tanya realigned her path from corporate leadership to purpose-led entrepreneurship. Prior to LITO creative, she held the role of vice president of marketing at Fontainebleau Miami Beach. In May of 2006, she was introduced to hospitality in Las Vegas at the MGM Grand, followed by a successful tenure as director of marketing for the Hard Rock Hotel in New York City, which she opened in 2020.

She previously served as director of marketing for Gansevoort Hotel Group, having led the team through a rebrand; as digital/CRM and brand marketing manager for Denihan Hospitality Group; and as marketing manager for W New York Union Square.

With globally recognized brands like LVMH and Marriott, she has launched various initiatives to drive brand equity, member loyalty programs, strategic partnerships, and entertainment talent representation within programs such as CFDA collaborations, Billboard's "Next Up" series, and "What She Said," a female empowerment series by W Hotels, NYC Global PRIDE in collaboration with Stonewall Foundation. She also holds and held an HSMAI award in advertising, digital marketing, and public relations for a brand campaign that increased RevPAR by fifty percent YoY and garnered over one hundred sixty million impressions for a single campaign with Denihan. Tanya has led property migrations through the SPG loyalty program to the Bonvoy member program, launched the first keyless pilot with Starwood, and launched the Unity members program for Hard Rock Hotels Worldwide.

Tanya lived in Hawai'i before relocating to New York and holds degrees from LaGuardia Community College in international business; New York University in media, culture, and communications; and the fashion institute of technology in product development and design.

LITO creative (www.litocreative.com)
Kalena Kai (www.Kalenakai.com)
Instagram: @Litocreative
Instagram: @Alohakalenakai

Where the Spark Began

Deanna DeRiso

During my junior year of high school, a teacher asked the class what we wanted to be when we grew up. Without hesitation—and without really knowing what it meant—I said, "an entrepreneur."

At the time, it was just a word that sounded full of possibility. I didn't realize I was speaking my future into existence—that one day, I'd build something rooted in creativity, connection, and meaning.

Some stories are written in gold—and mine is one of them.

My main job—owning a beverage distribution route—has always been something I'm deeply proud of. It's steady, fulfilling work that gives me the independence and flexibility to always be there for my daughter. But even with gratitude for that stability, I couldn't shake the feeling that something was missing. I had built a foundation—but I longed for spark. I needed something that reignited my creativity and joy, something that felt like me.

That spark arrived the day I discovered permanent jewelry— a modern, meaningful twist on personal adornment. Each delicate chain is custom-fit to your wrist, ankle, or neck, then hand-welded to stay on—a seamless, clasp-free piece that symbolizes strength, connection, and intention. Designed to be lived in—showered in, slept in, celebrated in—it represents something deeper than style. It's about moments, meaning, and the bonds we choose to keep close.

That concept—beauty that lasts, connection that endures— became the heart of Bond + Bella Permanent Jewelry.

The name itself carries generations of love. "Bond" represents connection—between friends, family, and the stories that shape us. "Bella" is especially meaningful—it's my middle name, my maternal grandmother's name, and my daughter's middle name. Three generations linked by love and legacy—a reminder that what we create can last far beyond ourselves. And through every chapter, my mom has been a constant source of strength and support, encouraging me in everything I've ever done and continue to do. She's the bridge between those generations—the quiet force reminding me that love, faith, and hard work truly build beautiful things.

My journey didn't begin in a studio or showroom. It began at my kitchen table, surrounded by tiny chains, tools, and the noise of everyday life—balancing motherhood, business ownership, and a creative dream. Every piece I welded, and every brand I've worked with, I've learned from. Each collaboration has shaped me—pushing me to refine my craft, elevate my vision, and stay rooted in authenticity.

From humble pop-ups to collaborations with brands like LoveShackFancy and WhoWhatWear, Bond + Bella has grown into something truly special—a brand rooted in meaning and built on connection. Whether it's a best friend duo linking matching bracelets, a couple marking an anniversary, or a mother and daughter bonding over something timeless, Bond + Bella is about more than jewelry—it's about moments that matter.

But beyond the gold and silver, this story is also about balance and becoming—the courage to chase something new while still honoring what you've built. Running two businesses and raising a daughter isn't always easy, but it's real, it's rewarding, and it's mine.

Today, Bond + Bella Permanent Jewelry is more than a brand—it's a reflection of my heart, my family, and my belief that the most meaningful things in life are made to last.

Because in the world of Bond + Bella, every chain tells a story—and every bond is forever.

The Vision Ahead

As Bond + Bella continues to grow, my vision is simple: I want to continue working with amazing brands—creating experiences and jewelry that their consumers will love forever. Every collaboration is an opportunity to connect with new people, celebrate meaningful moments, and share the magic of permanent jewelry in a way that feels personal and unforgettable.

My goal is to make every Bond + Bella experience—from intimate events to large-scale brand partnerships—something that leaves a lasting impression. Because when something is made with intention, care, and connection, it becomes more than jewelry—it becomes a memory.

And that's what Bond + Bella will always stand for: beauty, connection, and bonds that last forever.

About Deanna

Deanna DeRiso is the founder and creative force behind Bond + Bella Permanent Jewelry, a brand built on connection, craftsmanship, and meaning. What began at her kitchen table has evolved into a sought-after jewelry experience—blending timeless design with personal storytelling. With a background in business ownership and a passion for creativity, Deanna has collaborated with brands like LoveShackFancy, WhoWhatWear, Alice + Olivia, and Bloomingdale's, bringing her signature touch of elegance and sentiment to every event. Inspired by her daughter, her mother, and the generations of women before her, Deanna continues to create jewelry that represents lasting bonds—pieces designed to be lived in, loved, and cherished forever.

Instagram: @deanna02 @bondxbella

Yes Girl; It's Real
Lessons in Grace

Nicole DeVincentis

NYC is in my blood, and part of my heritage—just like Italian and Irish. I've lived here my entire life, and it is my culture. You spend enough time here, and you have no choice but to become feisty, fast, and fearless. And I am proudly all of those things.

When I was five, I got plucked out of my big, beautiful suburban house and dropped into my grandmother's one-bedroom apartment in Jackson Heights, Queens. What I thought was a weekend visit turned into... well, my new life.

That apartment was a sauna, and the plastic-wrapped couch reeked of Opium perfume and Aqua Net hairspray.

At night, I'd share a bed with my snoring grandmother and fall asleep to the lullaby of honking horns and someone yelling outside in a language I had never heard. Every day, I would ask my mom the same question: "Mommy, am I in a dream? When am I going to wake up? Is this real?"

She looked at me—lovingly, but very certain—and said, "Yes, my girl; it's real. Daddy and I are getting divorced."

I have a vivid memory of that time; it was the first time reality hit me hard. It hurt so much that my mind just refused to accept it. For weeks, I told myself it was just a dream, that any minute now, I'd wake up back in my real life, in my real bed, and everything would be fine again. Looking back, I realize now that this was my first defense mechanism: denial, with a little bit of hope.

My first lesson in reality.

I was raised as an only child by a single mother who hustled to make ends meet—and even at that early age, I started to follow her lead. One day in third grade, the principal called me into her office to discuss my "perfume business." It was Mother's Day week—so I knew it would be a very lucrative one! All the kids were buying perfume for their moms.

"Nicole," she said, "we appreciate your entrepreneurial spirit, but you can't sell things at school. And five dollars a bottle is very expensive... parents are complaining!"

What could I say? I made high-quality goods that she didn't value. Her loss.

I took my business elsewhere.

By high school, I had a tutoring business for the younger kids. I loved every part of it—the scheduling, the interaction, the cash flow. But mostly, I loved that it was on my own terms. The parents were grateful, the kids were kind, and there was mutual respect. That was the spark. The entrepreneur was born right there, between algebra lessons and allowance money.

When I graduated from physician associate school in 1997, I was offered a job in the emergency department of a hospital I had rotated through during my training. It wasn't my dream job, but I knew it would serve as a kind of residency in medicine and make me a better provider in whatever I specialized in later. I spent four years there and loved it—but it wasn't until I landed in dermatology that I found what I knew I was meant to do. Boom. That was it.

I loved all of it: the babies, the kids, the elderly, and especially the teens. Helping them with cystic acne—the same acne I'd cried over and refused to leave the house for as a teen—really touched me. Years later, I'd run into those same kids, now adults, glowing and confident, and they were so thankful. It hit me: I'd helped shape their self-esteem. That was the best feeling—and I felt another kind of spark. Helping people feel better about themselves!! Here we go... *this* was something I really felt passionate about.

The physician who owned this practice was horrific to work for, though. Every morning, I'd have to call my mom for a pep talk just to walk through the door.

"Keep your eye on the prize, girl," she'd say. "Look at the big picture."

Like clockwork, every day at noon, I'd hear drawers slamming, followed by: "I need a fork!"—over the intercom, like a toddler. When he was offsite, he'd call just to berate me: "It's already eleven a.m.—why have you only seen fifteen patients?" Meanwhile, I was seeing forty patients a day. No assistants of any kind, no support staff, just me and the front desk.

It took me a while to realize he was hiding me from the industry—he was not introducing me to reps, not letting me network. I had no future there.

As I started to master general dermatology, I became fascinated by the aesthetic side, which his office didn't offer. This was 2008—Botox had only been FDA-approved for aesthetics in 2002, Restylane in 2003, Juvederm in 2006. It was brand new. I took every course I could find, picked up part-time work at corporate mills, and learned everything on the job. Somehow—thank God—I got really good at it.

In 2010, I was recruited by one of the pharmaceutical companies to be a full-time trainer. Accepting that role was pivotal. I didn't know it at the time, but it shifted everything. It meant leaving my current practices and setting up weekend hours to see my patients. I committed to seven days a week. I started in January 2011.

The company's training was invaluable. I was in two offices a day—teaching, watching, learning from the best and worst doctors in the field. I learned what worked, what didn't, and what kind of environment I'd create when I had my own practice. I also gave birth to my daughter in 2011—eight weeks early, preeclampsia, emergency C-section. You know, never the easy route... but she was healthy and perfect.

The next decade was a blur of hard work, long days, and lessons learned. Oh—and that little thing called motherhood.

Becoming a mother gave me something I didn't even know I was missing: a second set of balls. It made me bolder, tougher, louder in all the right ways. Motherhood doesn't soften you—it prepares you for anything. It gives you fire in places you didn't know you had.

Then came 2020. The COVID shutdown. And somehow, the universe decided it was my moment.

At the very beginning of lockdown, a great friend and mentor offered me her retail space—a hair salon—to transform into my medical aesthetics practice. The space was perfect but needed a total gut and renovation. Everyone thought I was out of my fucking mind.

"You want to open an office *now*? Are you crazy?!"

It didn't stop me. I opened in November 2020. No furniture, no décor—just my injection chair, a mirror, supplies, and my loyal following of patients, some with me for nearly fifteen years.

Year one was shockingly successful. NYC was locked down, and people had nowhere to go, nothing to spend on, and plenty of time to stare at themselves on Zoom. But they didn't just come to look better; they came to feel better. To talk, to laugh, to cry, to connect. That's when it hit me: this business isn't just about beauty. It's about connection. Patients must, of course, leave looking better—but they must also leave feeling better.

My mother—my ultimate cheerleader—helped me hold it all together. As a single mom with full custody, I was it. No backup, no partner, no plan B. She stepped in with my daughter, and they were inseparable. Nana was more fun than I ever was—soda, candy, and convertible rides with the music blasting at school pickup.

NYC started waking back up. The business was thriving, and I was finally hitting my stride as both CEO and provider. I was learning everything I could about leadership, management, and growth—and loving it.

Then, completely unexpectedly, in October of 2021, just a month shy of our one-year anniversary, I sat at my mother's bedside in the ICU holding her hand. She had been admitted emergently the night before.

"Momma, please—you can text—it's so hard for you to breathe," I said, tears streaming into my mask. But she insisted on saying it out loud.

It took her a full five minutes.

"It's...lung cancer," she said, gasping for air between words. "A tumor—at the top—of my lung—pushing—into my throat. Spread to—my bones—liver—adrenals. They—gave—me—two—weeks."

I thought I was hallucinating. Just the week before, she'd been picking up my daughter from school, making her dinner as usual. How could this be?

Am I in a bad dream? Is this real?

Yes, girl; it's real.

Days later, I told my staff what was happening—that my availability would shift while I handled this. Within weeks, I found out one employee was working for a competitor on the side, and another was sleeping with a patient.

WTF. Talk about kicking someone when they're down.

But I had one saving grace—one diamond in the rough. A young woman I'd started training a year earlier stepped up and truly ran the show. She held it down without me even asking. She reminded me what loyalty looks like. My Work Ride or Die. She is still with me, going strong, and I am so proud of and grateful for her.

My mother opted for aggressive chemo. It was a seven-month roller coaster that ended with hospice at home with me and my daughter. I am grateful for every single moment. This may sound strange, but those months—in all their chaos and heartbreak—were some of the best times. We laughed, reminisced, and found beauty in the most ordinary things. She was incredibly graceful; even in dying, she was teaching me how to live.

When I finally came up for air, I went back to work like a woman on a mission. I rebuilt, rehired, refocused. The year 2023 came in like sunlight—I was lighter, freer, and finally breathing again.

There was a recurring theme, though. In a period of three months, four of my regular patients came in with the same news: they'd all been diagnosed with breast cancer by MRI. It felt like the universe was whispering. I was high-risk and already doing routine imaging, but I couldn't stop thinking about them and getting one myself.

So I got the MRI.

And I had breast cancer.

This can't be fucking happening. Now?! Can I have one year of smooth sailing? Is this happening to me? Is this real?

Yes, girl; it's real.

Life will absolutely kick your ass. It'll floor you, steal your breath, and then ask if you're done. But if you're paying attention, it'll also teach you exactly who you are.

And me?

I'm the girl who turned a third-grade perfume business into a hustle that never quit.

Who built a business in a pandemic.

Who held her mother's hand through her last breath and still showed up for her patients the next day.

Who got breast cancer and said, "Take them off. Let's keep it moving. I've got a life to live and a business to run."

So yeah—when life kicked my ass, I took notes. And every time I asked, "Am I in a dream? Is this real?" the answer was always the same: Yes, girl; it's real.

And I'm still standing. As always.

About Nicole

Nicole DeVincentis, MPA, PA, is a nationally recognized aesthetic clinician, entrepreneur, and founder of Glowtox NYC, a premier medical aesthetics practice in the West Village of Manhattan. With more than two decades of experience in dermatology and aesthetic medicine, she is known for her refined techniques, clinical integrity, and signature approach to natural-looking rejuvenation.

A board-certified physician assistant, Nicole earned her bachelor of science in physician assistant studies from St. John's University and her master's in health care administration from Long Island University. She is a fellow of the Society of Dermatology Physician Assistants and is licensed in both New York and New Jersey.

Nicole's work emphasizes individualized treatment plans that enhance each client's unique features while maintaining balance and authenticity. Her precision and artistry have earned her recognition as one of America's Top 100 Aesthetic Injectors, an honor that highlights her dedication to innovation and excellence in the field.

Through Glowtox, Nicole has built a boutique environment where science, artistry, and empowerment converge. She remains deeply committed to patient education, mentorship, and advancing the ethical practice of aesthetic medicine. Known for her expertise, warmth, and professionalism, Nicole DeVincentis embodies the modern aesthetic leader—combining skill, compassion, and vision to inspire confidence from the inside   out.

Instagram: @glowtoxnyc
www.glowtoxnyc.com

Becoming the Phoenix

Yasmin Elzomor

December 2015 was the moment that changed my life forever, only I didn't know it back then. I was far too busy creating my ten-year plan and trying to control every aspect of my life.

I was twenty-one, working three different jobs, and feeling financially on top of the world. I was in a relationship with a man I thought was "the one." My social life was exciting; I was attending the hottest parties and events thanks to my modeling career.

On the outside, everything looked perfect. But on the inside, things were far from perfect. I had a constant nagging feeling that something was off, that I wasn't truly fulfilled. But of course, I would shove that feeling down... after all, I had more "important" things to do, like make money and try to keep up with the hamster wheel of this matrix we live in. I mean, what would people think if I didn't have my life together? If I didn't fulfill societal standards? If I didn't live a perfectly curated life? Keeping up appearances was my priority, and there was no way I would surrender to my feelings of inadequacy.

Back to the moment that changed my life.

It was a cold, rainy December night. I was snuggling on the couch, watching a movie with my mom after dinner. I had just finished creating my vision board for 2016. I had so many goals and dreams I needed to achieve, and I was totally looking forward to 2016 being my most powerful year yet. Halfway through the movie, I started feeling this weird tingling sensation throughout my whole body. My vision started getting blurry, and my heart began to pound. *What in the world is going on?* I wondered. I was trying to take deep breaths, but felt like I was suffocating. I felt like I wasn't even in my body.

I started freaking out. My parents looked at me with fear in their eyes, trying to figure out what was happening. "I think you need to make an appointment with the doctor," said my mom with an urgent tone. I was hesitant because something deep down in my soul told me that this wasn't a physical issue. But I needed peace of mind, so I went ahead and found a holistic doctor, since I've never been keen on Western medicine.

The whole week leading up to my appointment, I continued to feel weird and disconnected. I didn't feel like myself, and I was riddled with anxiety. I tried doing things that brought me joy, but nothing seemed to work. Was I depressed? On the day of my appointment, I was nervous because I didn't know what to expect. I had gone years without going to the doctor or keeping up with my health, and I'd definitely ignored my body's signals. I didn't realize how out of touch I was with my body, so this felt like a major wakeup call.

The doctor called me into his office, and I immediately felt seen by him. He asked: "How is your soul feeling?" *Huh??? My soul? Sir, aren't you supposed to ask me about my vitamin levels and blood pressure?* The question caught me off-guard, and I responded with, "I don't know." Tears started to roll down my face. I felt like I was in a therapy session, and I didn't know how much I needed it.

After talking in-depth for about 15–20 minutes, the doctor gave me a solid plan to follow. "We're going to get your mind-body-spirit in alignment as they're all connected. We'll start with your physical body; I want you to begin a workout routine and stay consistent with your vitamins and holistic remedies. I want you to create more structure. Taking a few minutes out of your day to meditate is a must. Stop burning yourself out and take more time for recreational activities and be out in nature more."

Okay, I can do that, I thought. It would definitely be a lifestyle change, but at this point, I was desperate for help. No one else understood what I was going through or how I was truly feeling, so I needed to start somewhere.

Weeks went by, and day by day, I started feeling a little lighter. I was keeping up on all the things the doctor told me to do, and I felt physically stronger and proud that I was creating structure for myself. I felt this surge of momentum and motivation, and I slowly felt more and more confident in who I was becoming. For the first time ever, I felt so clear-headed. I was finally able to sit in silence and ask myself, "What's my purpose?" instead of running from my own thoughts and emotions.

Before "finding my purpose," I knew I still had work to do. I found myself feeling disenchanted with my friends, my hobbies, and my romantic relationship. I knew I had to start taking stock of the people in my life...and that was one of the most painful parts of this awakening process. It was time for me to face the hard truth: growth requires you to let go of people and old ways of being. My eyes started welling up with tears, and I could feel the grief creeping up to the surface. I knew it was time to get to work.

I started reading all the personal development books, listening to all the podcasts, and attending all the wellness and spirituality events I could find. I was relentless in my pursuit of understanding this new version of myself that was being born— and I wasn't planning on stopping until I got down to the truth of who I truly was.

Fast forward a few years, and I finally felt an unshakable inner confidence. I had days where I cried so hard because I didn't recognize this new identity. I didn't realize how accustomed I'd become to feeling small, insecure, and disconnected from myself. Shedding all these old beliefs and my old identity was one of the most painful things I ever had to do... but I did it because I knew if I played my cards right, it would lead me down the right path: the path of the victor. I came to the conclusion that I wanted to become a mentor and help others find their power and sovereignty. I had this newfound passion for all things personal development that I knew I had to help others unlock their potential through all the things I learned. I felt a sense of excitement, and for the first time in my life, I felt hopeful. The grey clouds that were looming over me were finally gone and the sun came out to play.

I'm in my early thirties now, and I've created my own empire. I wake up excited every day because I get to do what I love. I get to help people step into their most powerful selves, I get to be creative and discover different aspects of myself through my creative pursuits, and I get to grow and transform on a daily basis. Had I chosen to stay on the path of the victim, I would've never discovered the power that was hidden within me. The most powerful thing I discovered about myself had nothing to do with the superficial external accomplishments; it was about my inner accomplishments and my capacity to face myself and take responsibility for my life... that's the real gold. I rise not just for me, but as a reminder that transformation is possible, that the power is always within us, and that we all have the ability to start again—stronger, wiser, and unshakable.

About Yasmin

Yasmin Elzomor is a transformational guide, spiritual mentor, speaker, author, and podcast host of *Humanity Feels*. She helps people reclaim their power, embody their truth, and create freedom in love, intimacy, and life.

After a profound and sudden spiritual awakening at the age of twenty-one and a journey through heartbreak and self-reconstruction, she emerged from rock bottom with a fierce dedication to helping others alchemize pain into power and rebuild from their own destruction. With empathy, intuitive wisdom, and unwavering honesty, Yasmin guides people through deep inner work, helping them confront shadows, rewrite narratives, awaken to their sovereignty, and step into their true power.

More than a mentor, she is a visionary, alchemist, truth seeker, and creative force, leading with integrity and lighting a path for others to rise into their fullest potential.

www.yasminelzomor.com
Instagram: @yasminelzomor

Saying YES to Life's Perfect Recipe

Allison Fasano

I didn't know how I wanted this story to start, but I knew how I wanted it to end. You could say I'm just a chef, but the truth is, every single day—give or take a protein, vegetable, or starch—there are a lot of plates and moving parts. Such is life.

Food is more than nourishment; it is a reflection of the human experience. Each ingredient, flavor, and meal tells a story about who we are and how we live. In many ways, food mimics life; both are processes of transformation, balance, and connection. This story is a huge piece of who I am. It wasn't always delicious, but in the end, I found my perfect recipe, in life and the kitchen.

As I moved about in my career, I learned who I was as a chef, but most importantly, who I was as a person. Like most people, I had a vision of who I wanted to be but was far from this fantasy. I'm going to be quite frank with you: I never thought I had a voice or really stood for anything. But somewhere in my late twenties, I picked my head up. I knew in order to inspire and to make a difference, I had to do something that scared me. I also knew that, in order to put myself out there, I had to tell my story.

It all started with saying *yes*.

If you asked me about the biggest influence in my life, I would tell you my father. He served as a first responder at ground zero after 9/11. After being stationed down there for over a year, he was forced to retire from the NYC transit authority earlier than he wanted to. Eight years ago, at the age of fifty-nine, he passed away.

He was actually the first person to help me discover that I wanted to be a chef. For years, my father would sit and watch the Food Network with me, which was my biggest influence—most importantly, Rachael Ray. She did something I could only dream I could do: Let her walls down and let people in. She was such a great storyteller, was always herself, and she smiled for no reason. My father would often point at the TV and say, "Allison, someday that will be you that I'm watching."

At that time, I figured I would never end up there, but the person sitting next to me, the one who loved and believed in me the most, thought I could. Sure, my goal was to "make it" on TV, but it was mostly to be someone who made a difference. When I had any doubt, my father would always tell me, "You know, if you don't put yourself out there, no one will ever know you exist. "I never understood what he was telling me until he passed away. He was telling me to say *yes* to opportunities, to put myself out there, and to take risks.

His influence on me didn't end with his life; in many ways, it was just the beginning of shaping mine more deeply. I found myself channeling that same persistence in my own life, pushing through challenges, studying harder, and refusing to give up on myself, because that's what he would have done. Though he's no longer here to see the person I'm becoming, I live each day hoping to make him proud. In that way, he still inspires me every single day.

In the United States, fewer than seven percent of restaurants are women-owned or run by female executive chefs.[1] With a percentage so low, one might think it would make a female chef lose hope in a bright future. Instead, it inspired me to work harder and make my dreams a reality. For me, it's never about being a "female chef" or "male chef," it's just about being a chef, no matter the gender. Being a chef for me has always and will be about paying it forward and inspiring others, about being a teacher and an even better student. I've realized that I didn't need to be a TV chef to inspire people; I can do it on a daily basis right in my own backyard–which is really my own kitchen.

I've always felt like I work even harder when people tell me I can't do something. Life and luck favor the bold. If your actions inspire others to dream more, learn more, do more, and become more, you are a leader. Sometimes we do have to go where there is no path and leave a trail. We all have goals; maybe we are there already, or maybe we are still climbing that ladder. Either way, it's about instilling hope and success in others, and empowering people to accomplish their goals along the way. When making a decision and considering both outcomes, the *no* outcome is connected to regret, and regret is sometimes the biggest risk of all. The word *yes* is inviting and empowering. It's like saying, "World, I got this!"

Opportunity sometimes knocks gently and does not wait for perfect timing. The truth is, there is no perfect timing. Whenever you say *yes* to something, you gain experience. And with these experiences, whether good or bad, come valuable life lessons that help shape and build your character. Whenever I said *no*, it felt like I was missing out on something. That something could have been an opportunity to gain a valuable experience, learn

---

[1] Christina Troitino, "Less than 7% of US Restaurants Are Led by Women—One Director Wants to Change That," *Forbes*, February 29, 2020; Chef's Pencil Staff, "Share of Female-Led Michelin Restaurants Is Only 6%," *Chef's Pencil*, March 28, 2023.

something new, build a friendship, or simply learn a life lesson that could potentially help shape my character in an empowering way.

Saying *yes* is not something that always comes naturally... trust me, I know! I've said *yes* to things I truly felt I had no business being a part of. In most cases, I didn't even know these opportunities were even an option for me. Me, a keynote speaker? I would think never in a million years, plus what story do I have to tell that would be powerful enough to really affect people? Still, I did what my father told me to do. I said *yes*. I entered a world so foreign. I dove into the unknown and allowed myself to feel vulnerable.

For my first speech, I took a long time to ponder my topic. How could I captivate an audience when I felt as though I was the least qualified to be giving a speech, when I spend most of my days hiding in a kitchen searching for my next dish? So I decided to tell this story, about my father and saying *yes*. I realized my journey to "just say yes" could captivate an audience. I never feel like my story is enough, especially if you never tell it. Over time, I've gained confidence, and more so my voice. Now a five-time keynote speaker, I look for my next stage, a chance to make my impact.

I started saying *yes*, and it led me to places I would never have imagined.

And somewhere after I did my seventh show for the Food Network, I thought, *I guess my father was right...* and he was actually always right! At first, I didn't understand what he meant. Saying *yes* felt risky. It meant stepping out of my comfort zone, trying things I wasn't sure I could handle. But over time, his lessons began to shape me. My father's lesson wasn't about recklessness. It was about trust—in the world, in others, and most of all, in myself. Saying *yes* became my way of embracing growth, facing fear, and finding meaning in moments I might otherwise have missed.

Now, whenever I stand on the edge of something new, I still hear his voice: *Say yes.* You never know what doors it might open. Now, I search for reasons to say *yes*; it's never a *no* for me.

I'm excited for where every *yes* will take me. It has allowed me to make it to places I never knew existed. With every *yes,* I'm closer to that person I always wanted to be. So even if it shakes my voice, I say, *yes.*

I have created a lot of recipes in my career. I think the one my father helped me write might be my favorite. A meal, no matter how exquisite, must eventually be consumed and fade away. This fleeting nature teaches us to savor each moment, to appreciate the present before it's gone. In the end, food does not just sustain life; it mirrors it. Every bite holds a lesson in transformation, balance, and gratitude, reminding us that, like a beautiful dish, life is best when made with care, shared with others, and savored fully.

About Allison

Allison Fasano was born and raised in Williamsburg, Brooklyn.

She knew at eleven years old that she wanted to become a chef after seeing Rachael Ray on the Food Network for the first time. She began following and cooking alongside her father, who inspired her passion for Italian cuisine. Following her passion, she studied culinary arts abroad in Calabria, Italy, where she specialized in regional Italian cuisine. As a chef, Allison loves bold layers of flavor—food that tells a story, or what she likes to call *"Nonna Style"*—food that gives you a hug on the inside. Her passion and her dynamic personality landed her in the most exciting culinary scenes in NYC.

For over the past twenty-one years, Allison has worked in Michelin Star restaurants, including The Sagamore Resort, Lidia, and Joe Bastianich's Del Posto, and as a sous chef at Gato with Bobby Flay's team. Allison is a TEDx speaker, and her speech, "Food at Everyone's Table," illustrates the importance of food waste and how we can end hunger.

Allison has been a keynote speaker at the Athena Women's Leadership Award ceremony at Molloy College, a Hofstra

University Women's conference, and the Blazing Trails: Women in Business Summit, in Bozeman, Mont. She often speaks about her firsthand experience working as a chef, being a woman in the industry, and how she has often had to work even harder to earn the title. Her message, *Just Say Yes*, was inspired by her father, who served as a first responder at ground zero after 9/11. After his passing, she found herself following her father's advice and saying *yes* to things she never imagined. She hopes her talks inspire women to do things that scare them, because saying *no*, is the biggest regret of them all.

Allison has appeared on the Food Network's *Beat Bobby Flay, Chopped,* Fios' *Restaurant Hunters, Newsday FeedMe TV,* and *Dishmantled.* She recently won an episode of Food Network's *Supermarket Stakeout.*

Allison became the executive chef at Harleys American Grille in Farmingdale, New York, where she received a rare three stars. The restaurant was named one of the top five restaurants to try on Long Island in 2019.

During COVID-19, Allison fed first responders at COVID testing sites across NYC, getting them meals a day, which totaled over four thousand meals a week. When she's not cooking in restaurants, she gives back, often in support of the community and women. In March 2021, she raised thirty thousand dollars to help women-owned restaurants, and for young girls to go to culinary school and have mentorships.

She's currently a chef in Bozeman, Mont.

Allison's motto in life is: *"Food and laughter is what I'm after."*

Instagram: @ChefAllisonFasano

The History of My Life: How I Got Here
Ayo Fashina

It's funny how the smallest memories can shape your entire life. My first real lesson in style wasn't from TV or a magazine; it started in daycare.

I went to the same daycare as my three cousins, the girls everyone would later call *fashion-forward*. I was the sneaker-and-denim-shorts kid, carefree and rough around the edges.

Then one day, during *show and tell*, they walked in wearing matching patent-leather orange outfits with white church heels, glossy, loud, and perfect. We were aging out of daycare at that point, old enough to have opinions but still young enough to believe in glitter. I remember freezing in awe. It was like seeing a dream standing right next to me. That moment cracked something open inside me. I realized there was more to life than baking treats in my *Easy-Bake Oven*, playing *Bop It*, and dancing to *The BOX* music videos on TV.

What fascinated me most wasn't just how they looked; it was how *free* they seemed. Everyone's attitude toward them changed instantly. They had always been the "nerdy cousins," but that day, they became *the girls*. Everyone wanted to be around them.

My mom was relaxed but rooted in culture. There were things we didn't do and ways we didn't dress. Looking back, I realize that tension—the space between freedom and restraint—became the foundation of how I saw fashion. It wasn't rebellion; it was expression.

After that, I started small. Hair clips in my skimpy ponytail. Shirts tucked in. A purse I didn't need but wore anyway. I begged my grandma for jewelry every time she went to Nigeria. Those tiny changes made me feel like I had access to something bigger than me.

Early Lessons and First Stages

My mom, a single parent for much of my childhood, couldn't teach me about posture or powder puffs because she was busy surviving. So she put me in Barbizon, a modeling and acting school. It became my bittersweet dream.

I learned how to walk, how to smile on cue, and how to command a room even when my knees shook. Acting became my escape. I even auditioned for Disney once. I made it close but didn't make it in. Barbizon wanted checks, not dreams. Still, I took something from that experience: presentation, confidence, and presence.

Every Saturday, my mom and I went to Tysons Corner Mall. We would walk for hours, with her window-shopping while I studied everything around me. That was my introduction to actually being able to obtain fashion pieces in stores nearby and to think, in the fitting rooms, about what aligned and how I felt. That's where fashion became more than appearance; it became emotion.

Finding My Group, Finding Myself

Clothing became a fluent language. It connected me to people but also separated me in quiet ways. I loved my group, but I knew I wasn't meant to blend in. I wanted my clothes to say something even when I didn't.

High school was one long runway of identity: combat boots, North Face jackets, colored braids, Dooney & Bourke bags, lip gloss, and Sperrys. My best friend, who shares my birthday, and I used to go shopping every weekend. We didn't have much, but we made it look like we did.

And then, I met Olise. The pieces I wore without thinking twice, he thought they were art. I would be ready to move on to the next thing, and he would still be lost in the last outfit. I used to tease him, saying, "You can't come over until you confirm you bought my ASOS dress." It was our playful language, but looking back, it taught me something. He saw me in a way I hadn't yet learned to see myself.

Forever 21 and the Awakening

Junior year of high school, I got my first real job at Forever 21. It was my first taste of style, seeing how people planned their looks and styled pieces I already had in new ways. That store taught me creativity. I learned that luxury isn't about price; it's about presence. I saw women re-style the same shirt five different ways, and that taught me to see fashion like a puzzle.

I learned that you can also respect people's style even when you don't agree with it. I still appreciate the thought behind someone's perspective and the risk they take when it comes to fashion and personal style.

The College Years: Becoming "Too Much"

When I got to the University of Maryland, I was already walking with a different rhythm. On my first day, I showed up to class in a structured suit and floppy hat. Everyone else wore sweats and hoodies. The whispers started: "She's doing too much."

But I didn't care. I couldn't spend four years dimming my light under hoodies and sweatpants, pretending I hadn't just planned my outfit the night before.

The more classes I took, the better I dressed for the day. Weekends were for Georgetown, boutiques, window shopping, and long dinners at Lauriol Plaza. My cousins were already plugged into the D.C. fashion scene. One was at Georgetown University, surrounded by creative people who made style feel alive.

Zara had just entered our lives, a treasure chest for those of us who couldn't yet afford designer elevated designs but were still stuck on the local brands at the time. I would spend hours trying things on, learning fabrics, and feeling textures.

By then, my cousins and I were inseparable. We were the *it girls*, even if locals didn't understand it. When we walked into a room, people turned heads. Our energy spoke before our clothes did. We didn't need approval. We were living proof that you could own your space with grace and edge. And we were okay with the fact that only we understood it. We knew what people didn't know, so we kept our hidden gems to ourselves.

People used to tell me I should have gone to Howard, not UMD, that I "gave Howard energy." Maybe I did. But I was meant to learn how to stand out in places that weren't built for me.

The Pivot

I started college studying nursing but wanted art and fashion. I liked healthcare, but not the physical side of it. Watching people in pain daily broke my heart. My tolerance was low, and my empathy was too high.

When I told my mom I wanted to switch majors, she panicked. I understand now that she was scared. She threatened to pull me out if I changed. So I picked healthcare administration. It wasn't art, but it gave me structure.

After college, I tried everything, including two businesses that failed before I found my footing in assisted living management. I loved the purpose, the leadership, and the people, but deep down, I knew something was still calling me.

The Spark

Fashion wasn't a career goal; it was just my thing. Until one night, over dinner, Olise looked at me and said, "Why haven't you started a fashion page? This is what makes you happy."

I laughed it off. "It's too late."

He said, "Every time I see influencers online, I think, Ayo could do this."

That hit me hard because he was right. I had built my whole life around being safe, not fulfilled.

He told me Fashion Week was happening that month. "Let's go," he said.

I panicked. "Now? No invites, no plan, no outfits."

He just smiled. "We'll figure it out."

So we did. We took off work, packed what we had, and drove to New York. I taught him how to use a camera in the car.

In New York, I reached out to my cousin, one of the three, the one deeply embedded in fashion. She helped me navigate Fashion Week, and somehow, I got into three shows. Walking into those rooms, surrounded by people who lived creativity, I felt something click. This wasn't luck. It was alignment.

That trip changed everything.

The Turning Point

When I came home, I launched my Instagram page using what I already had in my closet. The feedback was overwhelming. People connected to how I restyled old pieces and mixed high with low.

That's when I realized my purpose wasn't to show people fashion. It was to teach them to see differently.

The Journey Continues

Since then, I've collaborated with brands I once dreamed about, attended Fashion Weeks, and built a small but powerful community that values authenticity over perfection.

What humbles me most isn't the growth; it's the support. People who've never met me tell me they feel me. They understand my passion before I even explain it. Some of them see me deeper than people who've known me for years. That's what love looks like in this space—being seen without saying much.

There are people who don't realize how deeply this runs for me, how much fashion is tied to my spirit. So when someone gets it, when they just know, it hits me right in the heart. Because it's rare to be known that way.

The Lesson

If there's one thing I've learned, it's that you don't need permission to start. You just need courage.

I've worked multiple jobs, failed, restarted, and rebuilt. But peace comes from pursuing what lights you up, even when no one else understands it.

Fashion has taught me patience, self-trust, and the power of expression. I may not have become the actress I once dreamed of being, but I realized I'm still performing, just through a different kind of storytelling.

Final Reflection

Style, to me, is faith in fabric form. It's grace wrapped in expression. It's showing up for yourself again and again, even when life says *not yet*.

This journey, with all its risks and reroutes, has been the most personal education I've ever had.

And truthfully, I've taken a lot of prerequisites not even mentioned here. The biggest one has been life itself.

About Ayo

Ayo Fashina is a DMV-born fashion visionary whose style journey has taken her from the corridors of the nation's capital to the curated streets of New York. With Nigerian heritage grounding her identity and a sharp eye for editorial elegance, she blends intention with risk—turning everyday dressing into an art form. Ayo began cultivating her style in high school, creating mood boards, thrifting, pushing boundaries, and refusing to dim her expression for the status quo. While earning her degree in healthcare, she interned with DC designers, absorbing the mechanics of fashion production, but always felt the pull toward creative storytelling through wardrobes.

When she made the leap into full-time content and curation, she brought with her not just stunning looks but a deeply personal narrative—crafting relationships, mentoring young women, and cultivating a voice that is both aspirational and accessible. Now based between DMV and NYC, she partners with bold labels, inspires "fashion girls" to dress with purpose, and continues bridging cities through sartorial storytelling.

Instagram: @ayofashina

Cracking the Ivory Tower: From Limited Too to *Vogue Italia* and The RealReal

Rachel Glicksberg

As the piercer brought the gun to my ear, I jumped up from the chair—not once, twice, but three times. Exasperated, she brought the gun up to her own heavily pierced ears and, in a blink, punched a new hole. "See? Not a biggie?" That extravagant gesture did the trick. Moments later, I left the store with two newly pierced ears. And she was right; it wasn't a big deal. I could absolutely do that again.

But let me back up. The year was April 2003. The location was the Newport Center Mall in Jersey City, N.J., a stone's throw from Hoboken, the one-square-mile town where I grew up. I was turning ten, finally having worn down my father to get my ears pierced for my big double-digit birthday. My mom, a busy psychologist with a Ph.D., took me for the big moment. I chose the store Limited Too, the utopia that was every Y2K pre-teen's dream—all glitter, bubble letters, popcorn shirts, and lava lamps.

Aside from these special mother-daughter trips and a subscription to *Teen Vogue*, my exposure to the fantastical world of fashion was brief. Growing up across the Hudson River from New York City, one of the world's fashion capitals, it should have been a no-brainer that this world existed. Yet, outside the confines of a mall store and a glossy magazine, I didn't know it.

Between soccer, softball, Girl Scouts, and Hebrew school, other shiny glimpses of this mystical world appeared. At ten, during a playdate, I sat with a friend's older sister and watched *Sex & the City*. New York. Big City. Fashion. Glamour. Dating. I was transfixed. Years later, it is still my favorite show.

The year 2004 brought the film *13 Going on 30*, with its premise of small-town girl Jenna Rink, played by Jennifer Garner, making a wish to be "thirty, flirty, and thriving." She instantly manifested into a thirty-something glamorous New York City fashion magazine editor with an apartment on lower Fifth Avenue. A few years later, 2006 gave us *The Devil Wears Prada*. I still remember the opening sequence: glamorous editors leaving their downtown West Village homes, hailing cabs en route to the office, juxtaposed against Anne Hathaway's clumsy Andrea Sachs. The fictional *Runway* magazine was based on *Vogue*, then operating out of 4 Times Square.

For high school, I was fortunate enough to jump across the Hudson and attend a small, progressive school on the Upper West Side of Manhattan. In May 2009, my father, who studied art history, took me to the Metropolitan Museum of Art's Costume Institute show, *Model as Muse: Embodying Fashion*. Coming from a family that valued the art world—my mother, in contrast, wrote off the fashion industry as superficial and materialistic—the art world felt like an acceptable gateway. I was struck by the sight of an Arthur Elgort photograph of a model next to a mannequin wearing the actual stunning outfit from the picture.

I spent my college years studying art history, interning at galleries in Chelsea. My studies focused on art history through the lens of fashion, examining the social, political, and cultural undertones of women's dress. In my freshman year, I applied for a summer internship at the Costume Institute, only to be rejected; the internships were intended for grad school and Ph.D. candidates. It wasn't until my junior year at my liberal arts school, just a short train ride from the city, that I landed an unpaid, for-credit internship at *Marie Claire* magazine. There, I experienced the fast-paced environment and the intersection of fashion and culture in the glossy magazines I had devoured. It was a perfect fit.

After graduation, I went to the local bodega and picked up every magazine I could carry. I realized that if I could figure out the email structure of a large corporation like Condé Nast or Hearst, I could essentially penetrate that mythical ivory tower. I went through the mastheads and cold-emailed everyone in the fashion departments.

This paid off. Alexis Bryan Morgan, the fashion director at *Lucky Magazine*, answered my email and agreed to an info session. Luckily, a position for a fashion assistant in the fashion closet had just opened up. After a handful of interviews, the spot was mine. It was a glorified internship, but it was a foot in the door. I was now working at Condé at the 4 Times Square location, rushing to work like the women I saw in *The Devil Wears Prada*, but I was more like Andy Sachs.

It was 2014, an interesting time in the changing landscape of legacy media. Eva Chen, the youngest editor-in-chief at the time, had recently been appointed to the helm of *Lucky*. The whispers were that the golden years of magazines—the '90s, with their enlarged spending accounts and drivers—were over. Layoffs were abundant, and magazines were folding or merging. Digital had not yet blown up; *Lucky* only had a couple of digital editors. Yet, unknown bloggers like Tavi Gevinson, blogs like *Into The Gloss*, and publications like *Refinery29* were pioneering the new landscape.

Just before the holidays, at twenty-two, after witnessing many rounds of cuts, I got the call that I was being laid off. Shortly thereafter, the magazine folded completely. Despite the instability, my time at *Lucky* fostered my love for emerging designers. The layoff was also the biggest lesson. I was able to witness the old guard of traditional media but knew I had to be flexible in my own path, given the changing landscape.

My sights were set on becoming a fashion editor, but the unstable landscape and the need to pay my bills led me to work for a small sustainable brand. The industry felt inaccessible, impossible to penetrate without deep connections.

It was during these years that I stumbled upon a *New York Times* article that altered the course of my career. It featured Sara Maino, head of talent at *Vogue Italia*, who founded the platform Vogue Talents dedicated to spotlighting emerging designers. Her quote struck me: "You will rarely see me at the big shows... I spend most of my time off the grid during show season, in dingy studios, classrooms—even people's living rooms. Many of the designers I am looking for don't have the money to come to me. So instead, I go to them." I felt an instant connection.

After a few bounced emails, I correctly guessed an address, and one morning, I woke up to a response from Sara. It essentially asked, "Can you write?" I had only done academic writing up to that point, but regardless, I replied, "Absolutely." Sara's trust wasn't immediate; it had to be earned, but the opportunity was on the table. My first pitch was on Bode, a then-unknown brand upcycling vintage fabrics into patchwork quilted pieces. It did the trick.

Suddenly, I was an early twenty-something with a key to the city. The *Vogue Italia* title opened doors. I cold-emailed PR teams and designers and soon started attending NYFW solo, meeting and interviewing designers. I wrote about the launches of Christopher John Rogers and covered indie designers like Sandy Liang and Collina Strada. I covered the student world through fashion schools and the CFDA (Council of Fashion Designers of America) initiatives, which led to writing for the CFDA as well. Being a solo agent, I immediately gravitated to the CFDA's young team, who were beacons of like-minded light in an intimidating industry.

In retrospect, being forced to be so independent was an extremely important career and life lesson.

In 2018, Sara introduced me to the team at 10 Corso Como, the Milan-based concept store opening its doors in New York. I led content for them on a contract basis, but this was a blip; the doors closed in 2020 due to COVID.

Around the same time, at the end of 2018, Noelle Sciacca, the kind editor I'd kept in touch with from *Lucky*, was starting a new role at The RealReal, the luxury secondhand marketplace. She was hiring, and I applied immediately. It's important to note that secondhand was not trendy then; shopping this way was a kept secret. Peers told both of us, "You're sure you want to go secondhand?" Years later, these would be the same people sending us their résumés.

I started in a junior role curating the online site's edits, but over the years, I raised my hand for more. I leveraged my network of designers and stylists and my relationships with top fashion universities and the CFDA. Now, almost seven years later, I lead the storytelling for the online site and sixteen retail locations, working closely with cross functional partners. I also lead our designer partnerships, and launched the company's upcycling program from the ground up. This program has turned into an unofficial incubator, serving as a launch pad to the CFDA/Vogue Fashion Fund. Emerging brands like Presley Oldham and Don't Let Disco are alums of our program and CVFF finalists.

It's been a wild ride to have started at the company pre-IPO, navigated COVID layoffs and store closures, and witnessed firsthand the secondhand industry's meteoric rise. It may not be a coincidence that for my college essay I wrote about the circular nature of secondhand clothing and the stories that our pieces hold.

A year or so into COVID, I moved into an apartment on West 12th Street. While hosting a viewing party for *13 Going on 30* for my 30th birthday, I spotted that the fictional Jenna Rink lived right down the block. Later that year, I peered out my window to see *And Just Like That*, the *Sex and the City* revival, filming in front of my building. My younger self would have gotten a kick out of that—that I had manifested my wildest dreams.

In the past two years, I've signed on to be a mentor for Monday Girl, the members' club for next-generation leaders. I was also asked to be a strategic advisor for Isle of Monday, a rental platform for rare vintage, and appeared as a guest on the *Fashion & Founders* podcast, spoke at SXSW, and moderated panels at New York City Jewelry week, among others.

I am now on the receiving end of an endless stream of coffee and informational interview requests. It is strange to be on the other side. My outlook has always been focused on the next mountain to climb, making it hard to reflect on how far I've come. "Me?" I sometimes think. Why would someone want to talk to me or seek my advice? It's difficult to acknowledge our worth. But just as Sara at *Vogue Italia* and Noelle at The RealReal offered me life-changing chances, I am determined to pay it forward to the next generation. I hope to do just that with Monday Girl, Isle of Monday, and any conversation with a fashion-hungry, ambitious hustler just starting their journey.

About Rachel

Meet Rachel Glicksberg, a New York-born, New Jersey-raised innovator dedicated to the intersection of fashion and technology—with a focus on sustainability—and fostering the next generation of creative talent. As the senior fashion and new initiatives strategist at The RealReal, the world's largest online marketplace for authenticated, resale luxury goods, Rachel is the driving force behind the editorial merchandising vision. She sets the content strategy and trend-based storytelling across the company's website and retail stores nationwide. Notably, she founded The RealReal's upcycling program and leads the company's designer partnerships.

Beyond her role, Rachel is a dynamic advisor and mentor. She advises the startup Isle of Monday, a rental platform for rare, designer, and archival vintage, and is a mentor for Monday Girl, a members club that supports women who are in the early stages of their careers. Her extensive background includes her time as a longtime contributing editor for *Vogue Italia,* where she covered the New York emerging designer market. She also led content at 10 Corso Como New York and contributed to the Council of Fashion Designers of America (CFDA). Rachel is deeply committed to supporting emerging talent and uplifting the women around her.

Instagram: @rachelglicksberg

The Journey That Built Me

Lauren Hitchen

If someone had told me, while I was growing up in a small town on the English-Scottish border, that one day I'd be living in sunny Sarasota—running businesses, raising a family, mentoring women around the world, and helping them travel smarter and build freedom through multiple streams of income—I never would have believed them.

Life has a funny way of taking you places you never imagined. My story has been full of twists, turns, and unexpected detours, each shaping who I've become today. And honestly, I wouldn't change a thing.

A Spark in the City

It all truly began in 2000, when my family and I first arrived in New York City. I'll never forget the awe I felt seeing the skyline rise before me—the skyscrapers glinting in the sun, the energy of the streets, and the beauty of the Hudson River as we took that stunning train ride from Poughkeepsie into the city.

Stepping into Grand Central Station for the first time, I was overwhelmed by excitement and wonder. I didn't know it then, but that trip would spark a lifelong love of travel—one that would someday become my business and my purpose.

The forever love I have for New York runs deep. There's something magnetic about the city—the way New Yorkers embrace their authentic selves with such confidence and honesty. I love that I get to work and grow there, to be part of the city's rhythm, its resilience, and its endless drive. Being able to hop on a plane and be in New York so quickly still feels surreal—it's a privilege I never take for granted.

Across the Pond and Back Again

In 2001, when I was just sixteen, my parents decided to move us across the pond to Sarasota, Florida. Leaving behind our little town for palm trees and sunshine was a shock to the system! Adjusting to a new culture, a new school, and a new way of life wasn't easy, especially with visa restrictions limiting where I could go. But those years shaped my strength and taught me adaptability.

By 2007, I had discovered my passion—fashion marketing— and I was accepted into Parsons in New York City. I can still remember the thrill of getting those emails asking if I could help out at Fashion Week, and the adventure of exploring the city on my own, getting lost in the bustle of Manhattan.

I felt alive—finally on my own journey, living my dream in the best city in the world, doing what I loved. And then—boom— life had another plan. The 2008 economic crash hit hard, and my parents could no longer afford the school. I had to return to the UK on my own, leaving my family behind. It was heartbreaking, but that moment taught me independence and resilience that would shape everything that came next.

Finding Love and New Purpose

Back in the UK, my aunt and grandparents helped me rebuild. I found work in healthcare, where I met my husband, Jonathan, in 2011. We married in Sarasota in 2013—a destination wedding that became my first taste of travel planning as I coordinated flights and accommodations for over forty family members from the UK.

I didn't know it then, but my love for travel logistics had begun. I even planned Jonathan's surprise bachelor party in New York City because I wanted him to experience that same magic I felt all those years ago.

After the wedding, we returned to our lives in the UK. I worked agency jobs that taught me adaptability, a love for networking, and the freedom to travel. I didn't realize it at the time, but that flexibility would later become the foundation of my entrepreneurial life. Agency work showed me that freedom—something that would come full circle later through the opportunities travel provided.

Motherhood and Strength

In 2015, we welcomed our beautiful son, Ethan. His birth was complicated—a traumatic cesarean and months of recovery—but it taught me to trust my instinct, a lesson that would guide me in every area of life.

When Ethan faced early health challenges, including laryngomalacia and seizures, I learned the power of advocacy and strength through adversity. Thankfully, he grew out of both conditions and is now a healthy, smart, and kind ten-year-old—with the cutest American accent that none of his friends can believe came from a boy born in the UK!

Ethan's first trip to New York was unforgettable—watching him learn to walk there, seeing his eyes light up as he climbed into his first fire engine, and letting him run free through the Smithsonian Museum of Natural History, soaking up every sight and sound. It reminded me why I fell in love with travel in the first place—seeing the world through his eyes.

Entrepreneurship and Evolution

By 2017, we were ready for a new start. Jonathan, Ethan, and I moved back to Sarasota—it felt like coming home. The beaches, sunshine, and community made the transition smooth.

We partnered with my brother, Will, in a commercial window cleaning business, which we still operate today. That leap taught us the highs and lows of entrepreneurship—adapting, leading, and persevering through challenges like visa issues and the uncertainty of 2020. Those years bonded us deeply as a family and gave us a new strength we still carry.

In 2022, after years of visa restrictions, I finally became a permanent U.S. resident—and that's when everything changed. A single Instagram message introduced me to the world of travel advising, and something instantly clicked. I threw myself into building The Jet Set Travel Group, helping families plan unforgettable journeys and mentoring women to build smarter, more sustainable lives through multiple streams of income.

Then, in 2023, my journey came full circle. Remember that dream of studying fashion marketing at Parsons? That passion came to life with Rosa Tierra, an online fashion brand I co-founded with my dear friend Catalina, curating elegant and sustainable pieces from Colombia and South America. Within months, we were featured in British Vanity Fair!

The Luxury of Growth and Freedom

As my business evolved, I began to find my niche in the world of luxury—blending my love for travel, freedom, and fashion into a seamless experience. What started as bespoke trip planning grew into something much larger.

The world of private jets soon opened up to me, and in 2025, I proudly entered the jet charter and brokerage industry, expanding our services to include luxury air travel. It felt like a natural progression—bringing together everything I had learned about elegance, experience, and exceptional service.

I've been lucky to be surrounded by an incredible group of people—entrepreneurs, dreamers, and mentors—who share a passion for travel and helping others. Together, we've built something phenomenal: a global community dedicated to empowering women to create freedom, wealth, and joy through travel.

Still Soaring

Looking back, I can see how every challenge prepared me for where I am now. I've learned that resilience isn't just about surviving—it's about thriving, even when the odds are against you.

America has given me so much: a beautiful community, lifelong friendships, and endless opportunity.

As I step into this next chapter, I feel more grateful than ever. Life isn't about avoiding the hard times—it's about learning from them and using those lessons to build something beautiful.

If there's one thing I've learned, it's that failure only happens when you stop trying. So here I am—still trying, still dreaming, still soaring, and still laughing along the way.

Here's to the journey—building, growing, and helping others create their dreams while exploring the world. I'm endlessly grateful for how far the journey has brought me—and even more excited for where it's soaring next.

About Lauren

Lauren Hitchen is an entrepreneur, mentor, and travel expert who helps women create freedom through smarter travel and multiple streams of income. Originally from the English-Scottish border, her journey has taken her across the globe—blending adventure, business, and empowerment into a thriving career that allows her to work from anywhere in the world.

As the founder of The Jet Set Travel Group, Lauren curates bespoke travel experiences, mentors others in building sustainable income, and leads a passionate community helping others see the world. She is also a jet charter and brokerage partner, connecting clients to luxury air travel with elegance and ease, and the co-founder of Rosa Tierra, a fashion brand featured in British Vanity Fair.

A lifelong lover of New York City—her favorite place for business, leisure, and inspiration—Lauren continues to inspire others to dream bigger, travel smarter, and live life without limits.

Follow My Journey
@laurenhitchentravel
@thejetsettravelgroup
@rosatierra_official

Faith as My Compass: From the Smallest State to the Greatest City

Stephanie Mattera

I grew up in the smallest state in the United States. Rhode Island, though small in size, is full of beauty, heart, family, and tradition. The beginning of my childhood was ideal, shaped by close-knit relationships in a small town, the foundation of an Italian-American family, and the joys of New England life, such as boating, beaches, and seafood. I was close to my grandparents. My maternal grandmother, Sarah, died of cancer when I was five and a half. My mother was her primary caregiver, and we were with her almost every day for the last year of her life. The time with her was a gift, and she is still vivid in my memory. My paternal grandfather, John, was also diagnosed with terminal cancer around the same time and died a year later. Without his stewardship, my dad's family began to fall apart.

From the age of six to fifteen, I experienced the separation of my parents, whose divorce would go all the way to the Rhode Island State Supreme Court. The case concluded in 1996. My cousins, who grew up with me like siblings, were also experiencing their parents' divorce. Sadly, the children had to choose sides in that divorce. Today, there is a term for it: parental alienation syndrome. I had limited access to most of them for the rest of our lives. My favorite cousin, Maria, would take her own life in 2007, and I believe this outcome was directly related to her early childhood trauma. Her mother, Linda, had been married to my dad's brother. While circumstances alienated Maria from her mother at an early age, I was fortunate to experience Linda's love and influence. My aunt planted seeds of faith in me, as a devout Christian, and this has been the greatest gift of my life, carrying me through adversity.

I was also blessed to have the example of a powerhouse entrepreneur and alpha female, Aunt Melanie, who was married to one of my dad's brothers. She built an iconic real estate brand. Melanie represented elegance, ambition, and leadership. Watching her succeed taught me that women could build empires while staying true to themselves. She didn't have children, and I remember thinking about that as a little girl. I understood that women could choose motherhood, motherhood and a career, or pursue a career without motherhood. All of those paths are options.

My mom is the primary influence in my life. She believes that how you present yourself to the world reflects how you see yourself. She always made sure I was well-dressed, even as a little girl heading off to school. She'd say, "If you want to do great things, start by showing up as your best self." That lesson stayed with me. Fashion, to me, became more than fabric and trends—it was a vehicle of communication. It was how I told the world who I was before I even spoke a word. Equally inspiring to me is my mother's selfless example of giving back. It isn't just about how she shows up for me; it's about how she shows up for everyone. She is the person friends and family rely on without hesitation. She gives without expectation, never seeking recognition or reward. Everything comes from her heart, and that quiet generosity left a lasting impression on me.

So when I moved to New York City—a place where I didn't know anyone —I carried her example with me. I realized I could build connection and purpose through service. Philanthropy became my way of living out the values my mother modeled. Through charitable work, I found my community.

I also had incredible teachers who encouraged my curiosity and nurtured my confidence. Their belief in me reinforced the idea that education is the key to empowerment, a value my mother instilled in me, too. God gave me each of these women to shape me in different ways. As I grow older, I often reflect on just how vital their examples are to me.

By the time I graduated from college, I was eager to learn about business, leadership, and the world beyond Rhode Island. I pursued an MBA in global business leadership. A decision that would become a turning point in my life. During my graduate studies, I strategically sought a career to bridge my academic training with my creative side, and that aligned with my passion for style, communication, and purpose. I knew I wanted to work in New York City, the global capital of fashion and opportunity.

I was offered a position by Macy's Merchandising Group as a product development executive trainee eight months before graduation—the result of years of hard work, planning, and prayer. I knew this opportunity wasn't just luck. I believed God opened the door for me, and it was my responsibility to walk through it.

At that time, my life seemed picture-perfect. I was twenty-four, about to finish my master's degree, in a loving relationship, and had a dream job waiting for me in New York City. It felt like everything was falling into place. However, life often tests us right when we think we have it all figured out. My relationship was serious, and I believed I had found "true love." He was kind, supportive, and grounded—a man who made me feel safe. His family embraced me, and for a while, it felt like our lives aligned. But when I received the job offer in New York City, everything changed. He didn't want to relocate. He felt the cost of living was too high and worried about going backward in his own career. For him, Rhode Island represented comfort and stability. For me, New York represented growth and destiny.

I agonized over the decision. I prayed for clarity, asking God to help me see the path He wanted me to take. In the stillness of those prayers, I realized that true love wouldn't hold me back from fulfilling my purpose. So, even though it broke my heart, I chose my career. I decided to step into the unknown, to leave behind what was safe.

Moving to New York City at twenty-five was both exhilarating and terrifying. I was a young woman from the smallest state stepping into one of the largest, most competitive cities in the world. The pace was relentless, the expectations high, and the challenges constant. Yet, through it all, I believed that God guided my path. He bestows unique gifts and talents upon us. It's our responsibility to nurture those gifts and use them to live our purpose and serve others.

Faith doesn't mean life is easy. I've faced disappointments, career obstacles, and personal losses, but in every single season, God's grace has carried me through. I've come to understand that God doesn't solve our problems for us. Instead, He equips us with strength, courage, and wisdom to overcome them. He opens doors, but we must have the courage to walk through them. When I look back on my journey from Rhode Island to New York City, from heartbreak to healing, from ambition to purpose —I see a tapestry woven with both struggle and grace. Every challenge refined me. Every setback redirected me. Every blessing reminded me that I was never walking alone.

Working in New York City for over twenty years has taught me more than I could have ever imagined. I learned to balance ambition with authenticity, style with substance, and independence with faith. I also discovered that fulfillment is about living in alignment with the purpose God placed inside of you. Over time, my faith has only grown stronger. The moments that once seemed uncertain now make perfect sense in hindsight. Each door that closed made room for a better one to open. Each loss deepened my capacity for compassion. Each success reminded me to stay humble and grateful.

Today, I still believe that fashion is a form of communication, but faith is the most authentic expression of who we are. Faith shapes how we carry ourselves when no one's watching, sustains us when life feels uncertain, and reminds us that no matter how far we go from where we started, we are never far from God's plan.

I often reflect on that pivotal moment in my twenties, the choice between love and career. I realize now it was never just about either. It was about choosing faith in myself, in my purpose, and in the divine path God prepared for me long before I could see it. Through the years, I've learned that faith is not about knowing how everything will unfold but about trusting that it will. Rhode Island gave me roots, New York gave me wings, and faith continues to guide me.

Because when you let faith be your compass, you never truly lose your way.

About Stephanie

Meet Stephanie Mattera—New York University professor, philanthropist, and lifestyle expert. She began working in New York City twenty years ago for a career in corporate fashion after completing an MBA in global business leadership. Stephanie's first role was in product development for Macy's Merchandising Group, and she was promoted within one year to teach the corporate curriculum and incoming product development trainees. In addition to working for several global lifestyle and fashion brands, she served as a *Glamour* brand ambassador for six years, appearing in print and digital advertorials and representing the magazine at events. Her last corporate role was in global communications and crisis management at Starwood Hotels and Resorts.

Ten years ago, she transitioned into academia to prepare the next generation of public relations and corporate communication practitioners to excel in the field. She leverages her industry connections to bring real-world client experiences into the classroom, including Veronica Webb, Save the Children, and Highclere Castle Gin.

Stephanie is well-traveled and loves Europe. The past two summers, she has been in the Côte d'Azur for the Cannes Lions International Festival of Creativity and Festival de Télévision de Monte-Carlo in Monaco and NYU Global Field Intensive with visits to the premier *maisons de couture* and agencies in Paris, France.

Instagram: @stephanieannmattera

Dr. Gab: Resilience in Red Lipstick
Dr. Gabrielle Ashley

My story begins on Long Island, where I was born and raised. Growing up, I faced relentless bullying and battled several chronic illnesses. I made a quiet promise to myself early on: I would rewrite my story. I wouldn't let the bullies win.

By the time I turned eighteen, I had two big dreams: I wanted to become either an actress or a doctor. Both seemed unlikely, but I figured I'd give each a fair chance and see which one would take hold first.

In my late teens, I began auditioning every chance I could. I spent weekends and summers on sets for films, music videos, and creative projects. While pursuing these opportunities, I was also studying pre-med during the school year, hoping to one day become a psychiatrist. College became my foundation—a place where I began to understand who I wanted to be and who I was becoming.

I fell in love with psychology almost by accident. I remember sitting in those early classes, completely enthralled by how the mind works and how emotion, biology, and environment intersect. As my coursework intensified, my acting took a backseat. I decided I'd keep acting for fun during breaks and dedicate the rest of the year to exploring psychology.

College was a period of transformation for me. I took every opportunity to expand my world, including studying abroad—but I didn't want a "typical" semester abroad experience. I double-dipped. First, I joined an immersion program in Madrid, Spain, and later another in Morocco. I wanted to learn Spanish—my mother's first language—because she hadn't taught it to me growing up. It was humbling to be in another country where I didn't speak the language.

Morocco, especially, changed me. I was mesmerized by the people, the rhythm of daily life, and the richness of their culture. I learned about gender roles, religion, and values from perspectives I'd never considered. The trip opened my eyes to the idea that if I ever wanted to truly understand people—as a psychologist or as an actress—I needed to understand the world.

That trip softened me. I had always been anxious and perfectionistic, but seeing how other cultures valued presence and connection changed something in me. I learned the Spanish word *sobremesa*—the time spent talking after a meal—and it stuck with me. In the United States, I used to eat quickly at my laptop. In Spain, I learned to slow down, to savor conversation, to pause. It taught me that stress doesn't create success—balance does.

Back at school, I began gravitating toward psychology research. I decided to approach a professor I deeply admired—though most of my classmates were intimidated by her—to ask if she needed research assistance. Her office was dimly lit, filled with stacks of papers and jars of preserved specimens, like something out of a Halloween movie. I nervously asked if she needed help on any projects, and to my surprise, she looked up and simply said, "Yeah, sure—here's what I'm working on."

That's how I got involved in her research on human trafficking with the United Nations. She told me stories of working with the CIA, religious leaders, and peace organizations around the world. I was captivated. She helped me apply for a grant to conduct research in a country affected by high trafficking rates—I chose Togo, West Africa.

When I told my parents, they were terrified. They begged me not to go, wishing I'd just do a typical spring break like everyone else. But I was determined. I packed my malaria card, my passport, and a sense of purpose.

Arriving in Africa was like stepping into another dimension. The sun was the largest and brightest I'd ever seen. The fruit was rich and abundant, the air alive with sound. I was fascinated by the alternative medicines and spiritual healing practices I witnessed—plant-based remedies, exorcisms, and rituals that revealed a profound connection between spirituality and health. It challenged everything I thought I knew about healing.

Returning home was emotional. I suddenly saw my life of running water, electricity, and healthcare access through a different lens. My research paper became a thank you letter—an offering to the beautiful people of Togo who had changed my worldview forever.

After college, I took a gap year as a case manager in New York City to make sure I was ready to commit to a doctorate in psychology. I graduated on a Friday and started work the following Monday. I remember walking through Times Square, amazed by the skyline and the sense that I was finally where I belonged. That job gave me some of the most powerful stories I've ever heard—the true heartbeat of New York.

Then, my world stopped. My mom—my best friend, role model, and biggest supporter—passed away suddenly from cancer. She was my everything. We never argued, and our bond was something that often left people in awe. When she died, I broke. I couldn't think, breathe, or feel.

Thankfully, I was surrounded by mental health professionals who held space for me in my grief. Two weeks later, I received my acceptance letter to a PsyD program in Boston. I wanted to call her so badly, but I couldn't. Leaving New York was painful, but I knew I had to keep going—for her.

A few months later, I packed my car and drove to Boston. At first, I hated it. Everything closed early, there were no late-night coffee spots, and as one of the youngest in my cohort, I struggled to find my place. But this was just the beginning of the next chapter of my story—where psychology, resilience, and purpose began to take on a whole new meaning.

Something resurfaced during that time—an old echo from childhood. I thought about why I had been bullied. I realized it wasn't just because I was different, but because I had dared to be confident. I wasn't part of the cool crowd, but I dressed like I belonged to myself. Even in college, professors would tease that I must be in the wrong class, that fashion was next door. I'd smile and gently correct them: "No, I'm here for science."

When I entered grad school, people warned me: *Don't expect to have a social life, don't expect to date, don't expect to have money—psychology will become your life.* I remember whispering to myself, *Not me.*

I made it my mission to do all of the above—to live fully, love deeply, and stay true to who I was. During my auditioning days, I had built a small social-media following, and I decided to nurture it again. It became more than a hobby; it was my bridge back to joy. Creating content helped me find community in Boston, meet inspiring artists, and keep balance amid the rigor of my studies. It even helped pay my bills.

Most importantly, it kept my mom close. In every photo, I wore something of hers—a ring, a barrette, a dress. Each post was a conversation with her, a quiet act of remembrance. She always told me not to back down, and in that creative space, I honored her voice.

For my dissertation, I turned inward—toward the very tension that had defined so much of my life. I wrote about female CEOs and the psychological double bind of women in leadership, exploring how femininity, confidence, and authority collide in professional spaces. Women are often told they're *too much* or *not enough*—too emotional, too cold, too confident, too accommodating. My research found that many powerful women shared this struggle, and in that realization, I found both validation and community.

I dedicated my dissertation to my mom—the strongest, kindest, most luminous woman I've ever known. Everything I am—my ambition, compassion, and fire—comes from her.

When I look back, every moment that once felt like pain—the bullying, the isolation, the loss—became the blueprint for the woman I am today. The girl who once struggled to fit in grew into the woman who no longer asks for permission to be both soft and strong, both analytical and artistic. I learned that healing isn't a straight line; it's a lifestyle.

Today, I'm proud to live a life that bridges both worlds—working as a psychologist treating trauma and addiction while also creating content that makes mental wellness feel beautiful and accessible. I've realized that fashion, wellness, and psychology aren't opposites. They're all ways of telling a story—of helping people feel seen, confident, and whole.

If I could tell my younger self anything, it would be this: one day, the very things that made you "different" will become your magic. Never dim your light to make others comfortable. You can be a scientist and a showgirl, a healer and a dreamer. You can study the mind and still love the mirror. You can be soft and still change the world.

Because the truth is—resilience isn't just about surviving. It's about turning your story into something radiant. And that's exactly what I plan to keep doing.

About Gabrielle

Dr. Gab (@doctorglamgab) is a NYC-licensed clinical psychologist specializing in trauma, substance use, and personality disorders. By day, she works in hospital settings and psychiatric units immersed in some of the city's most complex and emotionally demanding cases—from human-trafficking research to acute treatment on psych wards. Her work focuses on the psychology of resilience, emotional regulation, and the art of helping people rebuild their lives from the inside out.

After hours, she channels that same emotional intensity into creativity—expressing herself through fashion, wellness, and biohacking content that redefines what self-care looks like for the modern woman. Her platform is a visual diary of recovery and reinvention: a place where luxury meets longevity, and where mental health conversations unfold through style, movement, and self-expression.

From walking NYFW runways to modeling for major campaigns, filming on movie sets, or testing the latest wellness innovations, Dr. Gab merges evidence-based psychology with real-world glamour. Her content invites women to reclaim self-care as both a science and a ritual—blending clinical insight with aspirational aesthetics that make healing feel elevated, not clinical.

Through her lens, balance becomes the ultimate luxury. Her message is clear: recovery, resilience, and radiance can coexist beautifully in one life—and that's the true essence of self-care.

Instagram: @DoctorGlamGab

The Birth Story I've Never Expected to Tell

Audrey Mora

Big City Dreams

As a Native New Yorker, I've always been a workaholic and a hustler. The "city that never sleeps" isn't just a slogan—it's a rhythm that runs through my veins. I've always felt the need to stay busy, creative, and curious. Growing up in New York City, there's always something to do and endless dreams to chase. It's a city that teaches you that opportunity is everywhere—if you're willing to go after it.

From Fashion Sketches to Strategy Decks

My grandmother, Milagros, was my earliest inspiration. She owned two tailor shops in the Philippines at a time when it was rare for women to lead businesses—all while raising six children and caring for my grandfather after his early strokes. Her strength and creativity sparked my love for fashion and entrepreneurship.

As a nod to her, I followed her footsteps into style and design. I studied fashion history, researched trends, and taught myself to sketch. I even took classes at the Fashion Institute of Technology, but when it came to actually sewing... let's just say I was better behind the concept board than the sewing machine.

That realization led me to pivot to the business side of fashion. I attended LIM College to study fashion marketing, where I found my sweet spot: blending creativity and strategy. I minored in journalism, contributed to the school's newspaper and blog, and began building my online presence through my personal blog and social media. I shared local events, pop-ups, and snapshots of my personal style.

Those early digital days opened unexpected doors. I was honored to be named one of *Lucky Magazine's* Favorite Bloggers two years in a row, and even appeared on the red carpet at their Lucky Shops events. Around the same time, I was selected as one of *Project Runway* Season 10's featured bloggers, where I interviewed contestants and guest judges weekly. My two passions, writing and fashion, had finally collided, and I was watching my dream take shape in real time.

Fashion remained such a strong part of my identity that I'd often choose sample sales over dinner (no regrets). I interned at several Condé Nast publications, where I learned the true grit it takes to make it in this industry. My time there could have been straight out of *The Devil Wears Prada* (at least in my personal experience). Interns were often in tears, I'd have to carry gowns through the subway, and once I was yelled at for not finding a "gray" pair of boots that turned out to be pink. But I took it all in stride. I saw it as a rite of passage—the unglamorous yet necessary foundation that toughened me up and prepared me for everything that came next. To this day, I credit those experiences for my calm under pressure and ability to thrive in chaos.

At LIM, we were required to gain hands-on experience in the industry, which turned out to be one of the most valuable lessons of my career. During that time, I discovered a love for PR and marketing, and was lucky to learn from incredible mentors at TSE Cashmere (Alyson Day, Eddie Murphy, Tina Lutz). I later returned to TSE as their PR manager after graduation.

Those early years taught me everything, from scrappiness and creativity to the power of collaboration. Seeing our work featured in publications like *Vogue* and *WWD* was the most rewarding validation of our collective effort.

I eventually transitioned into hospitality, joining brands like Gansevoort Hotel Group and Hard Rock Hotel New York (a special shoutout to my mentor, Tanya de Costa, who saw and nurtured my potential). I even went full circle from interviewing Heidi Klum for *Project Runway*'s blog to designing one of her iconic Halloween party invites for Hard Rock. These experiences deepened my love for partnership building, community engagement, and food and beverage marketing.

Along the way, I've freelanced with PR agencies, luxury showrooms, retail brands, boutique designers, and even in real estate. As NYC teaches you, there is always the opportunity to chase your dreams.

From Chaos to Clarity: My Why

I'm incredibly lucky to have found my husband, Andres Mora. We met at a Battle of the Bands concert in 2008, and he's been my rock ever since—through every late-night project, job change, and adventure, all while gracefully handling my fiery and stubborn Taurus energy. Together, we have two beautiful girls, Beverly and Blaire.

In 2022, during Blaire's C-section delivery, I experienced an unexpected anaphylactic reaction. Moments after holding her for the first time, I suddenly couldn't speak, open my eyes, or breathe. Everything went dark. I woke up in the ICU, alive but shaken, and spent days recovering before reuniting with my newborn.

That experience changed everything.

It shifted how I see time, work, and what truly matters. Family became my focus. Stressful deadlines or small work setbacks no longer held the same weight because I learned firsthand how precious life really is.

Our healing journey afterward was necessary, but not easy. My husband suffered recurring nightmares for months after witnessing it all, and still has them occasionally. For me, it was mourning the idea of another child as I was torn between not wanting to risk putting us through that trauma again, and still longing for one more addition to our family.

I underwent months of allergy testing and consulted with multiple physicians, who reassured me that another pregnancy could still be possible with careful planning in the operating room. I even met with a medium to explore the healing journey spiritually.

Hustle & Heart

Through my daughters' eyes, I've learned to rediscover joy and see familiar things in a new light. I want my girls to find their own passions and joys. In doing so, I want them to discover what lights them up and pursue it with purpose. My hope is that they grow up to be independent, driven, and kind, with the same determination I've always carried, but also with the wisdom to pause, savor, and enjoy every step along the way.

That same outlook fuels what I share online. On my platform, I curate family-friendly activities, date-night spots, hidden gems across New York City, and exploring new destinations together as a family. My content is about living intentionally: making time for what matters, finding beauty in everyday moments, and celebrating both hustle and heart.

I hope you'll join me in this adventure.

About Audrey

Meet Audrey Mora, an NYC mom influencer and lifestyle content creator who turns everyday family adventures into a city guide parents actually use. With a career in the glamorous PR and marketing world, including time with publications at Condé Nast, Gansevoort Hotel Group, and Hard Rock Hotel New York, she brings a polished yet approachable perspective to parenting, lifestyle, and culture. Her content highlights family activities, date-night eats, travel, and book recs across New York City and Long Island—plus concerts, shows, and buzz-worthy pop-ups. Her community follows her for smart, kid-friendly finds and insider access to launches and cultural events.

After a traumatic delivery with her second child, Audrey realigned her priorities, embracing wellness, joy, and presence as guiding values—and being able to enjoy and rediscover an exciting life through her daughters' eyes. Today, she blends thoughtful reviews and meaningful partnerships with a genuine, family-first approach, always delivered with warmth, curiosity, and a true native New Yorker's eye.

Instagram: @audreyomora

Defy the Odds: Build, Transform Your Finances

Denise Muñoz, EA

Are you willing to push through adversity to achieve your goals? Will you defy the odds? I come from a background where sharing your personal story is discouraged, silence is often mistaken for strength. Thanks to Leigh, I found the courage to write my story. Not for recognition, but in hopes that it might inspire someone to defy the odds and secure their finances. Challenges do not determine your future. Adversity does not define you; you have the strength to defy the odds and be financially sound.

I was born on Tax Day in a quiet suburb just outside the buzz of New York City, in Rockland County. Years earlier, my family had emigrated from the Dominican Republic, forming a vibrant and loving community where even small moments felt like celebrations. Our family gatherings were special; they became a tradition, especially during the holidays. Moments were full of laughter, spontaneous shows with my cousins that turned the living room into a stage, and unwrapping secret Santa gifts. We had feasts that could rival any chef's; the food was a mosaic of different flavors, each dish lovingly prepared by a different family member; every bite told a story.

Although my childhood had its joyful moments, it was a rollercoaster shaped by circumstances beyond my control. These challenges forced me to mature quickly and become self-sufficient so I would not be a burden and could help my family. I began working at a young age, initially with my parents in their cleaning business, and assisted with cleaning and office work. Once I reached working age, I took on a formal job while continuing to support my parents' business and attending school. Managing my own finances became essential; it allowed me to cover some of my own needs and eventually fund my own path through college. While I would have loved to participate in more extracurricular activities, it simply wasn't feasible.

My teenage years were nothing like those of a typical teenage girl. They were years I never truly experienced, years that can never be returned. At that time, I met my former partner, who was five years older than me. What began as an introduction quickly turned long-term, far too serious for my age. It changed everything. These were years I should have spent living joyfully, like other teenagers, but instead, I was stuck in a volatile relationship and gave up on many of my dreams like modelling and dancing.

During the winter of 2010, my life shifted, and I was blessed with an amazing son. His arrival changed my outlook on life completely. He gave me purpose, strength, and countless reasons to keep going. Failure was not an option. I had someone depending on me, and I refused to give up, regardless of the circumstances. He came just a year before I was set to graduate college, and finishing my degree became one of the most significant challenges I would ever face. There were sleepless nights filled with studying, weight gain from stress, and the elimination of every distraction—no television, no events, no socializing, and very little time with family and friends. With the unwavering support of my family, I managed to juggle full-time college, work, and motherhood. It wasn't easy, many weekends were spent at the campus library studying, while missing precious moments with my little one. To manage it all, I strategized and organized everything, creating schedules and routines to keep life balanced between home, work, and college. Unwavering opinions emerged. Some people didn't believe that I'd be able to finish college and would focus solely on being a mom. The expectation was clear: a woman should stay home, cook, clean, and raise children. To me, that was outrageous. Becoming a mom wasn't the end, it was the beginning. It gave life more meaning and purpose.

Finally, in the spring of 2011, I graduated from Mercy University with a degree in public accounting. As the first member in my immediate family to graduate college. The story society tells that a woman with a child cannot finish college, succeed, and build a career is nothing more than an unrealistic opinion. My accounting career was just beginning, and I carried with me the strength of every challenge I overcame. Interestingly, years later, I'd become an accountant, and every April fifteenth feels as if the universe gave me a nudge toward my destiny.

Home was far from perfect. While there were joyful memories, many days were volatile and challenging. One evening, after returning from work, I noticed that one of my fashionable skirts was missing and my flip flops had been used. Confused and uneasy, I began my own quiet investigation. What I uncovered shook me to the core; while I was away, women were secretly invited into my home and using my personal belongings without my consent. It felt like I was living inside a *telenovela*, a real-life soap opera. It was the final betrayal. I realized I had been living a lie for years, losing precious time that could never be reclaimed. Slowly, I came to terms with the truth: this was unhealthy, stunting my career and growth, and it was time to leave.

Deciding to leave took several agonizing and scary months because of the consequences and challenges it could bring. Financially, we depended on each other, and I did not have enough savings to relocate my son and myself, as it was early in my career. What I didn't expect was how quickly things would unravel and how heartless someone could be. As I was saving for us to move, one day, I found some of my belongings stuffed into black garbage bags, and we were told to leave. That day is etched in my memory, marking the end of one chapter and the beginning of another. This new chapter brought a sense of anxiety with liberation, freedom, and empowerment after years of being restrained.

We then moved into a rented room in a relative's home, later into an apartment. The apartment was beautiful, yet I couldn't shake the unease of paying rent without building equity. It eventually led us to my family home in an effort to save and work toward something permanent. During that time, I was laser-focused on finding a way to earn enough to buy a home. That thought consumed me.

Future clients began asking me for help with their taxes and accounting. After coming home from my full-time job, I started working out of my kitchen, serving a handful of clients in the evenings. That was my lightbulb moment. I realized I could start my own firm. That was my defining moment. I realized it was time to build something of my own. After years of helping others build their businesses with my ideas and walking away with nothing, it was time to invest in myself. Over the years, word of mouth and referrals expanded my client base. Years after starting, I was able to achieve my goal: I bought a home and continued serving clients. When the coronavirus hit, I had to step out of my comfort zone and pushed to move into an office space that ultimately allowed me to expand further. Once I moved into my own office space, I realized that working for myself offered true security. Financial independence wasn't just a goal; it was the key to transforming my future. I knew I had to focus on building my firm. Then life took an unexpected turn: I was laid off from my job and what began as a side business became my main financial source. Over the past fifteen years, I've been working as an accountant in different industries, and the experience acquired over the years has allowed me to create an individualized service that translates the accounting and tax complexities to clients.

I encourage anyone to start their own business and add additional income; solely relying on a salary is a risk. Diversifying your income streams can secure your finances and independence. If you ever start a business of your own, here is a quick guide to help you begin. Each business is different, and every state has its own rules. In a world where do-it-yourself is encouraged, I advise you to consult with a financial and legal professional. First decide what type of business feels right for you. Second, create a business plan. Third, contact an accountant early; this saves headaches later. Fourth, choose a business name that you will love. Fifth, elect the right business structure with the guidance of a professional. Sixth obtain taxpayer identification. You'll need it before opening a business account. Seventh, research licenses and permits; don't skip this step. Eighth, consider patents and copyrights to protect your inventions. Ninth, create an operating agreement. Even if it's just you, clarity matters. Tenth, if you decide to buy a business, consult with an attorney.

Many women are rewriting their futures, opting to leave or stay out of the traditional workforce in exchange for autonomy and flexibility. Financial independence provides opportunities, options, security, and freedom to live life on your own terms, build, protect, and preserve wealth, without being constrained by financial dependence. Choosing independence by creating your own business makes you the chief executive officer of your life, removing limitations and replacing them with possibilities. Anyone can defy the odds, build their own legacy and secure their finances.

About Denise

Denise Muñoz is a devoted mother, entrepreneur, and accounting and tax professional with over twenty years of experience across various industries within accounting and finance. Passionate about empowering entrepreneurs to build, strengthen, and preserve their finances, she believes that achieving financial independence is an important tool that ensures freedom to live life on your own terms.

Denise obtained a bachelor of science in public accounting from Mercy University and is an enrolled agent admitted to represent taxpayers before the Internal Revenue Service. She has fifteen years of experience in accounting and tax and five years in finance and specializes in guiding small to mid-size businesses and entrepreneurs to build wealth, maintain compliance, and navigate financial complexities through accounting, tax, consulting, and strategic planning. She is a member of the National Association of Enrolled Agents, National Tax Preparer Association, National Society of Accountants, and several other professional organizations.

Denise has cultivated a wealth of experience across multiple sectors, including real estate, wholesale, retail, service, ecommerce, wealth services, family offices, finance, and investment industries. Working in the ecommerce industry, she has gained extensive experience in multi-state and international taxation. Working as a family office and wealth services accountant at a top public accounting firm, she has serviced family offices of ultra-high net worth individuals, providing comprehensive services to executives, entrepreneurs, and their businesses listed on Forbes Top 100–500. She managed a boutique accounting firm in New York, delivering tailored accounting and tax solutions to individuals and businesses. Her background in finance includes five years of loan underwriting, budgeting, credit analysis, and servicing.

Beyond her professional achievements, Denise is deeply committed to causes close to her heart. Advocating for the causes that resonate with her, such as those dedicated to children and educational engagement, she has contributed in various capacities to parent-teacher associations. Motivated by a genuine passion for helping others, she contributes to volunteering, philanthropic, and public service initiatives that create a meaningful impact within communities.

Instagram: @dm_accounting @__denise.munoz
www.dm-accounting.com
LinkedIn: Denise Munoz, EA

Passport to Perspectives
Lindsey Olson

Of all of my blessings, I can think of few more impactful than the privilege of growing up with two cultures. Growing up a dual citizen of the United States and Mexico, I learned the beauty of approaching the world with two sets of eyes, the richness of culture within a multitude of places, and a pragmatic understanding of the light and the dark within every nation. I learned that each country is an amalgamation of its virtues and flaws, its dark histories, and its hopeful futures, and that each place you visit will bring you a new perspective to attach to your own life at home. Now having visited fifty-two different countries, all fifty U.S. states, and twenty-two of the thirty-three Mexican states, the lens of duality that I grew up with has shaped my approach to experiencing each new place: with an open mind and heart seeking not just fleeting joy and adventure but a deeper understanding of the fortitude of its people. Throughout my travels, whether in the tiniest town in the middle of nowhere to a large, abundant metropolis, I've come to find that there is no location that lacks its own kind of magic.

My mother, born and raised in Mexico City, came to the United States in her twenties, eventually meeting my father in Seattle, Wash. Born and raised in Tacoma, I grew up shuffling back and forth between my home town and Mexico City, spending summer and winter breaks visiting family. My parents, imbued with the love of travel they passed to me, took me all over North America during my childhood, with my first cross-border trip to Whistler when I was only four months old. I can still remember road trips through Mexico shoving my parents, uncles, cousins, and grandparents into my *tio's* Volkswagen van that broke down at least every other trip, once stranding us on our way back from Mazatlán in Esquinapa, leaving us to all take the bus back to Mazatlán on New Year's Eve while stopping in every tiny town imaginable. You'd laugh if you knew the debacle in finding a hotel for the night.

My journey of visiting all fifty states started before I can remember. My father, the first in his family to graduate college, was a devoted University of Washington Huskies fan, planning our every fall around home and away games. Thus, I spent my formative years traveling throughout other Pac-10 states—California, Arizona, and Oregon—as well as to occasional games that took us as far as Ann Arbor, Mich. Our travels were not limited to football, however, as my parents' fascination for erudition took us throughout the Northeast and Southwest. By my adulthood, I'd already visited more than half of the states without conscious effort, so around age twenty-five, I decided I'd make it my quest, funded by my growing ad sales career. From solo trips to Little Rock, Burlington, Kansas City, and Charleston, to visiting the only friend from high school who had ended up in Omaha (Nebraska and Iowa in one trip!), I slowly chipped away until completing my journey in Alaska for my thirty-third birthday. What I learned is that the United States has something remarkable to offer in every corner and town square, whether it is the smallest town in Arkansas or New York City itself. I've fielded plenty of questions about why I would want to visit the so-called "fly over states" or Midwestern towns reshaped by changing times and globalization, and my answer is always the same: I've cherished every one of them. People, not attractions, make places, and approaching each destination with curiosity and positivity can make any place a wonder.

My first overseas trip found me in France in the fourth grade. I went to a Montessori school with a robust French program as a child, and it organized biannual trips for students and parents that explored not only France but Spain, Monaco, and Andorra. By high school graduation, I'd visited Italy, Germany, Czechia, the U.K., and a whole host of Caribbean islands on a couple of family cruises. It wasn't until my adulthood, though, that I truly fell for travel, particularly after a solo trip to Quebec helped mend a broken heart.

Today, some of my favorite places to visit include Japan, India, Albania, Hungary, Colombia, Romania, Tanzania, Australia, Cambodia, and Vietnam—and that's just a snippet of the fifty-two countries I've had the pleasure of visiting thus far. Of course, each place is beautiful and offers a surplus of historical and touristic sites, but perpetually, the people are always one of the best parts. I've been lucky that my fluency in three languages (English, Spanish, and French) has taken me far interpersonally throughout the globe, but oftentimes the interactions are even more special when I can't communicate in the same language. From the kindness of the Albanians that took a phone call with my Albanian super when I was lost driving by myself in the absolute middle of nowhere, to the Japanese folks I met who would straight up leave their business to walk me in the direction I needed to go, to the kind rural Slovakians who bore with me in my desperate attempts to ask for an ATM with early 2010s Google translate, these interactions have both shaped me and touched my heart in an indelible way.

And, to bring it back to my dual cultures, I've also seen that two cultures that seem entirely unrelated can be similar in the best ways—take the multicolored warmth of South Asian cultures paralleling what I've experienced with my loud, huggy, Mexican family. Additionally, the curiosity you'll see around the world from people who learn you're from the United States, for better or for worse, will delight and surprise you, whether it's having a group of more than fifteen Indian people ask to take a photo with you while shoving their child in your arms, or clarifying misconceptions of some of the United States' worst stereotypes to the Nordics (who truly do seem to have it all figured it out).

Ultimately, one of the greatest gifts my travels and ability to see the world through two cultural lenses has given me is the capacity to view the United States with a broader, less myopic perspective than those who are shaped by a single worldview. It is easy to see your home nation in monochrome: either it's the best place on earth, or the worst. My experience has informed me that it is neither, but rather a vivid amalgamation of triumphs and tribulations just as you'll find in any other place, even with varying specifics.

The past decade has been a difficult one for the United States, marked by division and disagreement, but I can wholeheartedly say that there are many blessings and privileges here that you won't find everywhere you go. Americans touch the world with a unique friendliness and bright excitement, a distinct smile upon eye contact that feels born out of the nation's character. The American optimism and confidence in the face of adversity is remarkable, and the innovation that comes from the diverse tapestry of its people is undeniably special. At the same time, the United States isn't perfect—as no place is—but being raised in two cultures and experiencing fifty others has left me ripe with lessons about how we might collectively do better.

Other nations are meaningfully surpassing us in socioeconomic equality, data-informed happiness rankings, communal warmth, cultural expression, tackling violence, and supporting their populace through things like healthcare, education, and social safety nets. Acknowledging this isn't an insult; it's an act of love. One of the best ways to care for your country is to insist that it can grow. The entire globe has a wealth of lessons for us to learn, if we only choose to listen. I'm grateful that my life began with an outside perspective, and my best wish for those reading this is that you seek out as many different ways of seeing the world as life allows.

About Lindsey

Lindsey Olson is a Mexican-American travel content creator and software sales executive based in Brooklyn. She has lived in Seattle, Arizona, New York, Mexico City, and Philadelphia. At age thirty-three she completed her quest to visit all fifty US states. She has also explored twenty-two of thirty-two Mexican states, fifty-two countries, and six continents. She is trilingual in English, Spanish, and French.

Through her content, Lindsey aims to educate about the places she visits, highlighting history, fascinating facts, and cultural insights. Each caption shares unique aspects of cities, states, or countries, fostering genuine curiosity and learning on social media. Her favorite countries to visit are Japan, India, and Mexico.

A history enthusiast, Lindsey specializes in U.S. presidents, British monarchs, and the Romanovs. She can name all the presidents in order in under a minute, and can share fun facts about any president from one to forty-five.

Lindsey also placed eighth out of eighty-one contestants on season one of Fox's *The Floor*, hosted by Rob Lowe. Starting with the category of Political Candidates, she won her duel and went on to defend the U.S. States category. Fun fact: she met her partner, Tom, on the show, who was defending the category of Bands.

You can find Lindsey on Instagram and TikTok at @linzolson

Leaping Outside my Comfort Zone

Susanna Paliotta

If there is one truth that has shaped every chapter of my life, it is this: success is never a single moment—it's a series of choices, sacrifices, and reinventions. I was not born into wealth, nor did I begin my career with a handbook for entrepreneurship.

I was born in an era when deals were sealed with handshakes, where you could buy fruits and vegetables from local farmers and leave cash in a tip jar with complete trust. It was a world without Instagram or Facebook, a time when building a network meant meeting people face-to-face, looking them in the eye, and earning their respect. You couldn't google someone to verify their character—you relied on instinct, intuition, and word of mouth. Those early experiences shaped the way I approach business to this day.

Breaking Barriers in Business

When I first stepped into the world of business, I discovered something quickly: education alone didn't guarantee success. What mattered just as much—if not more—were resources, relationships, and the ability to build a strong network from the ground up.

I also realized early on that as a woman, especially one with big ambitions, I would have to work twice as hard to earn half the recognition. But instead of discouraging me, that reality pushed me harder. It awakened a drive in me that refused to settle. I became relentless in my pursuit of excellence. I took on challenges I was told I wasn't ready for. I walked into rooms where people didn't expect me, and I made sure they remembered my name when I walked out.

Over the years, my ventures have stretched across multiple industries—from fashion to aviation, philanthropy to media. Some of those businesses flourished beyond what I ever imagined. Others humbled me and taught me lessons that success never could. Through every high and low, my commitment to innovation and impact remained my guiding force. Business, to me, has never been just about making money; it has always been about creating something meaningful.

Fashioning a Brand with Purpose

Entering the fashion industry was one of the most transformative chapters of my journey. Having the ability to build three successful companies alongside my daughter, Isabella Barrett, has been one of the greatest highlights of my fifty-three years on this planet. There is something incredibly meaningful about creating not just businesses, but a legacy, hand in hand with your own child.

Together, we learned, we hustled, we failed forward, and we pushed each other to rise to every challenge. Watching our ideas turn into thriving companies—and then seeing two of those businesses grow strong enough to be acquired by major corporations—remains one of the proudest and most defining accomplishments of my entire career. It wasn't just about the success; it was about proving what determination, teamwork, and family can achieve when they move with purpose and passion.

Aviation: Learning to Soar Beyond Comfort Zones

Venturing into aviation was a leap far outside my comfort zone—and that was exactly why I pursued it. When people hear the word *pilot*, they don't usually imagine a woman who looks like me. But breaking stereotypes has been a lifelong mission of mine. I never wanted to live in a box built by someone else's expectations.

Learning to fly required precision, discipline, and courage. It demanded trust—trust in the aircraft, in the training, and most importantly, in myself. Every time I took off, I felt a sense of freedom but also responsibility. Aviation pushed me beyond my fears and taught me that limitations are often illusions created by doubt.

While flying is just a hobby for me, it also reminds me to take time for myself and do things I truly enjoy. Maintaining my own identity outside of being a businesswoman, a mom, a wife, and so many other roles is incredibly important—not just for me, but for all women.

Reality Television and Media: Amplifying My Message

My introduction to media and reality television wasn't driven by a desire for fame. It was about visibility, representation, and using the exposure as a kind of commercial for my brands.

My daughter Isabella was actually the first in our family to become a TV personality—landing a starring role on an iconic show that instantly boosted the visibility of her brand. Five years later, it was my turn. When NBC Universal comes knocking, you don't hesitate—you answer.

Becoming one of Bravo's *Pageant Housewives* was an incredible experience. And after years of Isabella doing TV shows, press, and media, I had already built an impressive Rolodex of contacts. I leaned into those relationships as I pivoted into public relations, turning years of networking into a new chapter of opportunity.

Television taught me the importance of authenticity. My experiences allowed me to connect with a larger audience and amplify causes close to my heart—especially women's empowerment and children's advocacy.

Public Relations and Advocacy: Success with a Deeper Purpose

Throughout my career, I've devoted myself to helping other women grow, offering creative business strategies, branding support, and the kind of mentorship I wished I had earlier in my own journey.

What began as personal PR work for small businesses quickly evolved into something far bigger. In 2016, I landed my first major client: The Teen Choice Awards. That opportunity became my turning point. From there, my PR work expanded rapidly, taking me from Coachella Festival gifting suites to White House events, and nearly everywhere in between. I found myself partnering with influential brands, celebrities, global organizations, and entrepreneurs who trusted me to amplify their stories.

Public relations became more than a career—it became a mission. I learned how powerful visibility can be, how one well-placed opportunity can transform someone's entire trajectory, and how important it is for women to support one another in industries where doors don't always open easily.

People often ask me how I balance everything—my career, the media world, philanthropy, advocacy, and personal growth. The truth is, balance isn't a destination; it's a constant practice. And the greatest practice of all has been motherhood. My daughters taught me the value of grounding myself, staying present, and remembering why I push so hard for my goals.

They are the reason I continue to advocate, elevate, and build with purpose.

Looking Forward

My journey is far from over. There are new businesses to create, new stories to tell, and new communities to uplift. I am constantly evolving, constantly learning, and constantly seeking ways to make a deeper impact. The future excites me because I know I will continue shaping it with purpose, passion, and determination.

If there is one message I want to leave behind, it is this:

Your dreams are valid. Your story matters. And no matter how many times life tests you, you have the power to rise, rebuild, and redefine your future. And that, above all, is what makes a woman truly successful.

About Susanna

Susanna Paliotta is a successful entrepreneur, public relations agent, pilot, and television personality based in Manhattan, New York. She first came into the public eye as a housewife on Bravo's *Game of Crowns*, where her business savvy and charm shone alongside her entrepreneurial daughter Isabella Barrett.

A co-founder of House of Barretti, Susanna helped build a children's and teens lifestyle clothing brand that blends elegance with modern trends. Beyond the world of fashion, she's also a licensed small-plane pilot who loves flying her Cessna 172—a passion she attributes to her late father, an engineer and former jockey.

Susanna is an accomplished PR agent working for all the top award shows producing gifting suites and pop ups for names like Teen Choice Awards, The Oscars, BET and MTV Awards, Coachella, VS PINK, and more. Family is central to her life; she has two daughters, Victoria and Isabella.

While both girls are successful in their own right, younger daughter, Isabella Barrett, is a child actress and model who became one of the youngest self-made millionaires in the United States after selling a company she made famous at six years old.

In the pageant world, Susanna has held several titles—including Mrs. Nations USA, Mrs. Massachusetts Perfect Woman, and Mrs. Rhode Island United States—reflecting both her poise and her commitment to empowerment.

Financially, Susanna made the top five hundred women in business to watch by *Forbes Magazine* through her entrepreneurial ventures and television work.

Susanna Paliotta embodies a multifaceted career: she's a business leader, creative designer, dedicated mother, and activist—a modern renaissance woman blending glamour with purpose.

Instagram: @susannapaliotta123
Facebook: Susanna Paliotta
www.houseofbarretti.com

From Four Walls to the Seventh Continent: The Journey to Finding Oneself

Seemona Rahman

The sound of the ship's engine changed first.

It was a deep, resonant groan that slid under my skin. I was standing on the deck, wrapped in so many layers I could barely move. All I felt was the thrum of anticipation. I had just turned twenty-five and had flown from New York to Buenos Aires to the end of the world—Ushuaia, Argentina—all for this.

But the ship was turning. Not *toward* the ice, but *away*.

A collective gasp sucked the thin, frigid air from the deck. A man beside me raised a trembling hand as if to physically stop the vessel's momentum. "I have been waiting all my life for this," he said, his voice cracking.

I felt the ache of a dream breaking. It was a sharp, physical pain in my chest. This wasn't just a detour; it was a technical failure. The ship, with all our hopes still clinging to its frozen rails, kept turning.

That year, I did not set foot on Antarctica. I flew back home, but as the sting of disappointment faded, it was replaced by a cold, hard resolve. I learned something crucial: a dream deferred is a dream *tested*.

The very next year, at twenty-six, I was back on a ship. And when the churning gray waters finally calmed and I opened my eyes ... there it was.

Antarctica.

It wasn't just white. It was a thousand shades of blue, a piercing, ancient, electric blue. It was the sound of silence so profound it felt like a presence, with the majesty of gargantuan glaciers and mountains that seemed to hold up the sky.

Standing on the seventh continent, I felt insignificant, yet truly, utterly, remarkably alive.

The Walls of *Biyer Por Jeyo*

That moment of arrival was the culmination of a life spent pushing against walls.

I was born and raised in a well-known, traditional family in Bangladesh. I was loved and protected, but my world was small, my future a pre-written script. The world "out there" wasn't safe for a girl. The path was clear: education, yes, but ultimately, a good marriage, a family.

I might have accepted it. But my family spent a few of my childhood years in Stockholm, Sweden, where I saw women riding bicycles alone, their laughter open and unchaperoned. That glimpse of a different world planted a seed of impossible longing.

As a girl from a conservative Muslim family, there is a phrase that rings like a death knell to ambition: *"Biyer por jeyo."*

"Go after you are married."

It is the answer to every dream. "I want to study abroad." *Biyer por jeyo.* "I want to travel." *Biyer por jeyo.* "I want to live on my own." *Biyer por jeyo.* Your life, your identity, your freedom, are all things to be handed over to you by a future husband.

I am, to this day, profoundly grateful to my parents. Because when a life-changing opportunity came—a full scholarship to a boarding high school in Scandinavia, a program led by Nelson Mandela and Queen Noor of Jordan—they *didn't* say I had to wait.

They were terrified, though. I was a teenager, and the school was by a remote Norwegian fjord. I would be alone, thousands of miles from home. They stalled. They worried. The first month of classes ticked by without me. I pleaded. I reasoned.

In one last, tearful phone call, trying to convince my father, I said the only thing I could think of. "I am a soldier," I told him.

They let me go.

Those years in Norway were like breathing for the first time. It was the people—students from over eighty countries—who changed me. We were a kaleidoscope of cultures, and the friendships I formed were a new education. I learned that the world was not something to be feared, but something to be *known.* I even had the unfathomable honor of attending the Nobel Peace Prize Ceremony in Oslo when Dr. Muhammad Yunus and the Grameen Bank received their prize. I was a world away from the four walls of my childhood, and I knew that I could never go back.

The Soldier and the Plan

My parents' reluctant trust in me had shown them I didn't need a husband to survive. But this was only the beginning.

After Norway, I came to the United States for my undergraduate studies at the University of Wisconsin-Madison. But the ghost of The Plan followed me: finish my degree, go back home, marry a good Bangladeshi man, and raise a family. I was so driven by this invisible deadline that I completed my bachelor's degree in just under three years, graduating with the highest distinction.

I was packing my bags. I was ready to go home. The Plan was on track.

And then the letters came.

Fellowship offers for graduate school. Yale. Columbia. Cornell.

I held the thick parchment envelopes in my hand, my heart hammering against my ribs. This was not The Plan. This was a deviation. This was a choice. I could hear the phantom whispers of *Biyer por jeyo* all the way from Dhaka.

I thought to myself, *Now is not the time to go back.*

I chose the Wharton School of Business at the University of Pennsylvania, one of the most prestigious business schools in the world. It was an act of defiance, not just against my family's expectations, but against the girl I was raised to be.

Life soon brought me to New York City. At first, the city was a monster. It was too loud, too fast, too indifferent. But I found my first home in Greenwich Village, and in its crooked streets, I fell in love. New York was my Soul City.

Love, Aroha, and a New War

At twenty-seven, on my honeymoon in the impossible blues of French Polynesia and the staggering greens of New Zealand, I found out I was pregnant.

I had never felt so much love. It was a seismic shift, a reordering of my entire universe. Life, which I already thought was boundless, suddenly felt filled with even more possibilities.

But then, the chorus began again. Not from my family this time, but from friends, acquaintances, societal expectation.

"Well, that's it." "Your traveling days are over." "Now that you're a mother, you have to settle down."

The walls I had spent a decade tearing down were suddenly being rebuilt around me, this time as new, suffocating expectations. I felt a familiar panic rise.

In that moment of doubt, I remembered the girl who stood on a frozen deck, vowing to return. I remembered the teenager who, with a trembling voice, told her father, "I am a soldier."

My daughter, Aroha Rahman, was born. I named her after the Māori word *aroha*, which means, "love, compassion, and a life force that connects all things." She did not end my traveling days. She became my best travel buddy. She proved to be my wings, not my anchor.

With her by my side, I didn't just see the world; I *experienced* it anew. We swam with flamingos in Aruba. We chased the ethereal pink of cherry blossoms in Japan. I heard her shriek with joy as we ziplined through the jungles of Costa Rica and ran through the colorful Gamla Stan in Sweden, the place my own journey began.

I never stopped taking solo trips, either. I found myself bungee jumping into a double rainbow at Victoria Falls in Zimbabwe. I lived with zebras in Zambia and was woken by giraffes in Kenya. I danced with my best friend on the streets of Cuba and hiked my beloved Norwegian mountains once more.

Aroha didn't close the world off. She opened it.

The Ripple I Didn't See Coming

I was just a woman traveling. First alone, then with my daughter. But women in my own New York neighborhood, the Upper East Side, started to notice. I became their unofficial travel advisor. Then, the pandemic hit. The world stopped.

Trapped within my *new* four walls, with no traveling to do, I finally did what they had been asking. I started my travel blog on Instagram, @seemona.rahman. It was a lifeline. A way to travel through my memories, to connect with a world that suddenly felt very far away.

And then, the messages started.

"I finally went on my first solo trip!" "My baby is six months old, and thanks to your very helpful post, I am now planning a trip with her." "I saw your post, and I am so inspired to start planning a trip to Antarctica."

That. That is the power of influence. My small story of defiance was rewriting the scripts for other women.

This realization became my new path. I took my joy in empowering women and turned it into a profession. I started my own public relations firm in New York, Seemona Digital. I would help the brands I loved, the hotels I stayed in, the tourism boards of the countries I adored, reach their full potential. It was a new battle, breaking into an industry dominated by incumbent seniors, but I was a soldier. I made a space for myself.

The Oath and the Open Sky

And just like that, one fine morning in New York, I found myself in a large, solemn room, my right hand raised.

It was Constitution Day: the culmination of a journey I could barely comprehend. As I stood there, about to take the oath, all the years flashed before my eyes.

I saw the little girl in Bangladesh; the terrified, determined teenager on a plane to Norway; the student in Wisconsin; and the young mother, holding her baby, vowing that her world would only get bigger.

Tears streamed down my face as I spoke the words. I was a citizen of Bangladesh by birth, a citizen of Sweden by chance, and now a citizen of the United States by *choice*.

Today, I am a global citizen. I am all of these women. I have traveled to one hundred twelve countries across all seven continents, and my only dream is to explore more of this amazing, boundless world.

To the girl who has just arrived, clutching a visa and a heart full of impossible dreams: I see you. The path is not just long; it is *everything*. It will be hard, and you will be tested. But when you follow your dreams, when you push against the walls, when you decide to be your own soldier... it is the most rewarding journey of all.

Where to next?

About Seemona

Seemona Rahman is a New York-based entrepreneur, digital marketing strategist, and recognized international travel expert. She is the founder of Seemona Digital, a specialized public relations and digital marketing agency that serves clients in the travel, tourism, and lifestyle sectors.

Seemona is truly a global citizen—born in Bangladesh and having spent her childhood years in Sweden, she's now proud to call New York home.

Seemona pursued her higher education in the United States and attended the University of Wisconsin-Madison, where she graduated with distinction, earning bachelor's degrees in both mathematics and economics. She subsequently completed her graduate studies at The Wharton School at the University of Pennsylvania, obtaining a degree in applied economics.

While her academic background informs her strategic approach to marketing, Seemona is most widely known for her extensive global travel. She has cultivated a significant public platform by documenting her voyages to over one hundred countries across all seven continents.

Her professional focus centers on the luxury travel and lifestyle segments. A key objective of her work is to advocate for global exploration and to enhance the visibility and representation of South Asians within the international travel community. Through her agency, she provides strategic consultancy and marketing services, collaborating with a portfolio of leading hospitality, tourism, and lifestyle brands.

Instagram:
Seemona @seemona.rahman
Public relations firm @seemona.digital
www.seemonarahman.com

Unstoppable in the City: How a Native New Yorker Ignored the Naysayers and Found Success on Her Own Terms

Ellen Silverman

I grew up as an only child of a single mother in New York City, a fourth-generation New Yorker surrounded by strong, independent women. I lived with my mother, and my aunt and grandmother lived within two blocks of each other in Chelsea; together, they shaped every part of who I became. They worked tirelessly: my mother was a nutritionist at several leading Manhattan hospitals, my aunt was an accountant for a fashion company in Lower Manhattan, and my grandmother worked for Macy's for forty years.

My great-grandmother arrived in Ellis Island in 1905 from Warsaw, Poland, with four children in tow and nothing but determination. She settled on the Lower East Side, like so many immigrants did back then. My grandmother started working at age fourteen in the Garment District, and my mother was raised by her grandmother, continuing the chain of women supporting women. I learned early on what grit looked like and what sacrifice meant.

While I got my strong work ethic from these women, I felt enormous pressure to succeed. Independence became my armor. I wanted to chart my own course, to live without anyone telling me what I should be or do. Everyone around me worked so hard to give me a future—but that future didn't always feel like my own.

I was fortunate to attend a prestigious progressive grammar school in Greenwich Village, Bank Street School for Children, which supported creativity and original thinking. It was the perfect school for someone like me—curious, restless, and constantly asking *Why?* However, after eighth grade, everything came to a screeching halt. I didn't do well on those standardized tests that private high schools required for admission, and it seemed the door to a "good" education was closing fast. My family refused to consider public school, so I figured I would spend a year (at age fourteen) working for Macy's, thanks to my grandmother's influence and connections. Even so, I loved the idea of earning my own money. I opened a bank account as a teenager and enjoyed watching my money grow.

By pure serendipity, an elite prep school on the Upper West Side, Trinity School, announced in *The New York Times* that it was admitting girls for the first time. My aunt knew someone on the Board of Trustees, and I got in. The school was seeking a diverse group of women, and I fulfilled the Lower-Manhattan-progressive-school, middle-income demographic perfectly. In 1971, the girls at Trinity had to wear a specific uniform. My mother took me shopping for the traditional Trinity Blazer, a Dress Gordon skirt, and loafers at Lord & Taylor. It was quite a change from the blue jeans and tie-dyed T-shirts that I wore at Bank Street. The experience was far from idyllic—socially it was difficult—but it was an education in more ways than one. It introduced me to the world of privilege and wealth and opened my eyes to how people from culturally diverse backgrounds could coexist in the same school and city.

I ended up earning passing grades in English and history thanks to extra tutoring, which honestly did nothing for me. But I had to have this tutoring because the school principals were worried that I would never get into a good college. My family did everything Trinity told them to do, and they never listened to me; at the same time, I was getting straight As in math. It was no surprise that I was drawn to math. English and history classes left me cold—I didn't relate to what I was reading, and teachers often assumed I had reading disabilities and was a slow learner. I wasn't. I was just plain bored. Math, on the other hand, made sense. It was logical, fair, and precise. I thrived in it, even as I struggled elsewhere.

Trinity divided the students into five academic levels, and I was placed in the "dummy" level. But with determination and the unnecessary tutoring, I proved everyone wrong. I earned a scholarship to Carnegie Mellon University, majoring in math and business—my moment of redemption! I remember telling the headmaster that I got in. He was shocked since I was slated to attend a low-level women's college in Boston.

After graduating college, I earned an MBA in statistics and launched my career on Wall Street. I worked as an equity analyst, then a fixed-income analyst, and later as a technology consultant. I loved the energy of the markets, the fast pace, and the intellectual challenge. But as time went on, especially after the 2008 financial crisis, the joy began to fade. The work became arduous, the hours long, and the environment exhausting. I stayed in finance longer than I should have, since I had those golden handcuffs of a stable job and a great salary.

Yet another interest was quietly taking root. During my years in finance, I bought and sold two apartments, and that process fascinated me. I went from a three-hundred-fifty-square-foot rental in Lower Manhattan to purchase a huge pre-war apartment in Upper Manhattan for forty thousand dollars. In 1995, everybody thought I was crazy for moving so far uptown, but I knew that the neighborhood was going to appreciate. And it did. I sold the apartment for three hundred thousand dollars, six years later, and then purchased a Riverview co-op on the Upper West Side for three hundred ten thousand. After nine years on Riverside Drive, I sold that apartment for four hundred thousand and bought into a new condominium development in Harlem for four hundred twenty-five thousand. I plan to sell this apartment this year for close to one million dollars.

I have always had an instinct for spotting neighborhoods on the rise and properties with investment potential. Work colleagues were always asking me for real estate advice, and I realized that real estate combined everything I loved: design, finance, and intuition. When I was laid off in 2016 during a corporate restructuring, I took it as a sign. I was fifty-nine, and for the first time, I felt free. I got my real estate license and joined Compass, a company that mirrored my own values— forward-thinking, data-driven, and entrepreneurial. The transition felt natural. After years in finance, real estate didn't intimidate me—the challenge for me was learning to run a business and how to deal with people! I learned very quickly that people get absolutely irrational when it comes to investing enormous amounts of money. Buying or selling a home is rarely just financial; it is deeply emotional. People project their hopes, insecurities, and identities into their homes. Learning to navigate people's personalities taught me patience, compassion, and how to take the high road when emotions ran high.

Over the years, I have built a niche working with first-time buyers and international investors who appreciate my honesty and deep knowledge of New York City. I understand how this city breathes—how its neighborhoods evolve, what gives a building its character, and how timing shapes opportunity.

Looking back, my path might seem unconventional, but it has always followed two themes: freedom and independence. I have always loved being my own boss, creating my own security, and reinventing myself as the world evolves.

Growing up in the sixties and seventies, entrepreneurial endeavors were not something society encouraged—especially not for women. Back then, the message was simple: get an education, find a stable job, stay there until retirement, and then, maybe, enjoy your life. No one talked about entrepreneurship or risk-taking. It just was not part of the culture. Today, there are many ways for young people to work independently and become entrepreneurs. We have the technology; we have so many apps on our phones that can help us within minutes.

I also draw inspiration from women who are still working, such as Bobbie Brown, Bethenny Frankel, Gwyneth Paltrow, J Lo, The Kardashians, Madonna, Oprah, Martha Stewart, Jane Fonda, and Diane von Furstenberg—women who never stop reinventing themselves, no matter their age. They remind me that success is not about titles or power; it is about curiosity, resilience, and the drive to keep learning and adapting.

The societal standards of the baby boom generation that I grew up with have been completely turned upside down. One does not need the best education to succeed when technology and artificial intelligence are at our fingertips. Today, the world changes too quickly to depend on institutions or employers for stability. True security comes from knowing that you can build, rebuild, and thrive on your own terms. That belief runs so deep that I've included a gift in my will to support entrepreneurial students at Carnegie-Mellon University. I want future generations—especially young women—to feel empowered to create their own opportunities rather than wait for permission to succeed.

So that's my story—a story of independence, reinvention, and faith in what's possible when you trust yourself.

About Ellen

"Finding your sanctuary in the city that never sleeps" is Ellen's promise to all her clients. Whether her clients are seeking that perfect space or selling a prized property, she is fully dedicated to meeting their needs and protecting their best interests in the unique and vibrant New York City market. Ellen approaches every client interaction as a partnership, emphasizing clear communication and hard work to achieve common goals.

She has worked in real estate since 2016, after a seasoned career as a Wall Street analyst. Her excellent financial and analytical skills, command of the digital space, and organized and detail-oriented processes help her navigate all facets of real estate transactions. Born and raised in Manhattan, she went to Trinity School prep school, then graduated from Carnegie-Mellon University with a BS degree in business administration and mathematics, and also received an MBA from Zicklin School of Business.

Ellen has experienced living in New York City as a renter, buyer, and seller and therefore understands the ebbs and flows of the market and the diverse neighborhoods of Manhattan. Ellen has earned the coveted Certified Buyer Representative and Master Certified Negotiation Expert designations. In addition, her keen eye for interior design and staging and up-to-date insights into new condominium developments, bring greater value to her clients. Ellen serves both local New York City and Miami clients and international investors from Spain, Portugal, Italy, France, Austria, Israel, Japan, China, South Korea, Taiwan, and Vietnam.

https://ellenjsilverman.com/
Instagram: @ellenjsilverman

Born to Leave New York

Roxana Baldovin

There's a lot to be said about nature versus nurture. Growing up in the "greatest city in the world"—the City that Never Sleeps—means living in a constant state of restless motion. In New York, ambition is the air. You're taught to chase dreams that seem just within reach, especially when everyone you know is either a nepo baby or best friends with one. To be born and raised in the Big Apple is to be fluent in gluttony, luxury, and hustle. Which is exactly why I had to leave to be reborn.

From the moment you can read a subway map, New York teaches you that leaving is betrayal. The city feeds you a single narrative: this is the best place on Earth, and anywhere else is a downgrade.

"New York is the most sophisticated place in the world, Roxy," my mother would remind me whenever I suggested going away for college—as if sophistication were the end-all be-all to a fulfilled life.

But what is sophistication without lived experience? I wanted to taste all the flavors life had to offer, and then decide for myself. My Sagittarius moon and five life path might explain the wanderlust, but it was my NYC private school education that gave me the first push to dream big and wander far.

I was fifteen when I walked into the cafeteria, fuming about the news that my school had just turned down the offer to film *Gossip Girl* in its hallways. A bright light beaconed in the form of a table filled with pamphlets from different cultures. A Spanish chef making paella, a Thai family smiling with elephants. An eco-adventure in Australia with the Great Barrier Reef. I had decided I'd live with a host family in Orroroo, Australia. Population: 568.

My mother had little faith that separation anxiety wouldn't get the best of me—I had gone home early from sleep-away camp every single year. But this felt different. I wasn't just playing archery with a bunch of kids from Long Island. I was going to sleep under the stars and hear dreamtime stories from the Indigenous Australians. This was my first taste of native culture—and it felt more spiritual and connected to my soul than anything I had ever heard in Abrahamic religions.

The following summer, my best friend Jane joined me on another Experiment in International Living—this time, in Japan. That trip became one of my life's greatest early teachers. Culture shock was immediate: my host mom insisted on five a.m. runs, Sunday school was "optional" but frowned upon if skipped, and our family conversations happened through a flip-screen translator. Even in 2008, my host siblings' social lives existed entirely through screens.

My closest friend that summer was Grace, a free-spirited girl from Vermont who could quote Charles Bukowski and Hunter S. Thompson and knew every Red Hot Chili Peppers lyric. She had done mushrooms and acid—she told me *I* needed to do mushrooms and acid. A week after we returned to the States, she visited me in Brooklyn, and we ended up going on a psychedelic journey in Jane's backyard. I sat cross-legged as I watched my friends who would leave for college in a couple of weeks strum their acoustic guitars. I had never seen so many stars in the usually light-polluted sky that surrounded us. For the first time in my life, I felt immense gratitude, simply for the experience of being alive.

Leaving the cocoon made me appreciate my own. For as much as I thought Grace's rural Vermont upbringing tripping acid in the mountains was so cool, she felt the same about my stoop kid drinking forties and going to loft parties lifestyle. You don't have to leave your own country to experience a different way of being—just hop on an Amtrak, and it'll feel a world away.

After meeting Grace, I knew more than ever I had to go away for college. Los Angeles was always the end goal, but why not live somewhere I'd never live other than these four years? I read *On the Road* by Jack Kerouac and wanted to march to the beat of my own beatnik drum, so while everyone was sprawled across the Northeast, I set my sights on America's sexiest, biggest party school: Arizona State University.

Until that point, my life had been one long dichotomy. I grew up sandwiched between Sheepshead Bay and Brighton Beach, just down the boardwalk from Coney Island. This little trifecta of neighborhoods I was raised in is like nowhere else in the world. Not only was I surrounded by the Atlantic Ocean but by immigrants, too. After the fall of the Soviet Union in 1991, my little corner of Brooklyn became home to the largest Russian-speaking population outside Eurasia. Very few of my neighbors weren't Russian. We were Kazakh, Uzbek, Armenian, Latvian, Georgian, and like my mother, Ukrainian. She'd been raised in Poland, a Soviet Bloc country but not quite Soviet—an apt metaphor for my entire existence. I never fit neatly into a single box, which might explain why I've spent my life coloring outside the lines.

The concept of the American Dream had been my lullaby since before I could even say my ABCs. America was a place where you can be anything, and I intended to test the limits. My time abroad had made me fearless, adaptable, and ready to jump in full throttle to living three thousand miles away full time. I knew leaving New York would only expand me, and that home would always live inside me.

As much as I loved Arizona, it only made me that much prouder to be from "the most sophisticated place in the world." It was in Arizona that I realized just how special calling Brooklyn home was. New York City is a microcosm of the world. When you meet someone new, it's common to ask *What are you?* And no one raises an eyebrow. In Arizona, people were not only offended but confused because for the first time in my American life, most of the people I met weren't first-generation something. But New York City's a little Pangea—cultures from all over the world are gathered in one place. We are all first-generation something. Aside from my fellow Soviet comrades, my best friends were Indian, Colombian, Trinidadian, Puerto Rican, and Dominican.

Now what does all this have to do with the life and career I've built for myself?! Your experiences in life shape you into who you are. I had gone from a place where every person around me knew a few words in Arabic, Spanish, and Russian and Bengalis were easily distinguished from Punjabis to a school where my peers had never even heard of borscht and made fun of me for the curry in my refrigerator.

Those early contrasts shaped the artist I became. At the Walter Cronkite School, I studied broadcast journalism with dreams of becoming the next Anthony Bourdain—traveling the world, connecting culture through story. But as destiny would have it, I was blessed by the gods of music videos. Besides diversity, Brooklyn also had diversity creative talent.

There was a new wave of hip-hop on the scenes, "third-eye rap." It was targeted at other young adults who considered themselves to be Indigo children. We all received downloads from Source (aka the Universe) while high on mushrooms and

DMT. We aptly believed in a higher consciousness and spreading the message of the light.

My first music video ever was for The Underachievers. When I met them, they had ten thousand views. Our first video, "Gold Soul Theory," got twelve million. I quantum leaped into a new stratosphere of existence. Overnight, I became a living, breathing artist with a camera, a vision, and a purpose.

I always knew that was the life for me, but to be your own boss and discipline yourself is the ultimate test of *How bad do you want this?* I applied for every photo and video gig I could find on Craigslist. I told every ambitious musician I knew I'd do their video. The video that got my caged little birds to start singing all over the world ended up being for The Underachievers ft. Portugal the Man. The track name: "Amorphous." We shot the video in my office, and it was because of this video I was able to leave that office.

Soon, I founded PANGEAN, inspired by Richard Branson's empire-building spirit. We produced viral music videos under Pangean Vision while designing sustainable streetwear our artists wore in our videos. I forgot to mention the "we" I've been referring to consisted of me and my ex-boyfriend. When the relationship collapsed, so did our company—but not the skill set, and definitely not the drive.

Since then, I've directed viral videos around the globe, carved out a niche in the reggaeton and dembow world, and earned the nickname Señora Directora. Now, I'm developing my first feature film, set in my ancestral homeland, Poland.

I may have left New York, but New York will never leave me. New York gave me the wings to fly, and then dared me to use them.

About Roxana

Meet Roxana Baldovin, the visionary director behind your favorite music videos. Maybe you've seen Doja Cat's "Tia Tamera," G-Eazy's "Tulips & Roses," or Latto's "In n Out"—that's all Roxana's magic. With nearly a billion views across her work for Maluma, Steve Aoki, Wiz Khalifa, Lil Uzi Vert, Rico Nasty, H.E.R., Kehlani, and Snoop Dogg, she's the creative force reshaping visual culture. From Disney campaigns to Flaming Hot Cheetos commercials, her vibrant aesthetic has dominated screens worldwide. This Brooklyn-raised first-gen American was hand-picked as one of nine directors from six thousand applicants for HBO's *Project Greenlight*, pitching a million-dollar movie to Issa Rae and Kumail Nanjiani. Since being on TV, she's hosted red carpets and joined the renowned Groundlings improv troupe. She's even taken her talents to the stage—where she wrote, directed, and starred in her own one-woman-show, MANIC, playing fourteen characters.

Self-dubbed the "Spiritual Spielberg," Roxana brings her boundary-pushing vision to close out *Slaying New York* with the same energy that made her videos cultural moments.

roxanabaldovin.com
Instagram: @senoradirectora

About the Curator, Leigh M. Clark

Four-time best-selling author Leigh M. Clark is known for her inspiring books, including *The Dream is in Your Hands*, *Living Kindly*, and the *Slay the USA* series. Her work as an author has empowered and motivated countless readers by highlighting kindness, resilience, and the strength of community. In addition to her writing career, Leigh has over 20 years of experience as a business strategist, working with Fortune 500 companies to help them grow and succeed.

Leigh's latest project, the Slay the USA series, is a growing national movement that shines a spotlight on extraordinary women across the country who are leaving their mark on their communities and industries. Through this series, Leigh is empowering these women to share their stories of triumph, leadership, and impact, much like she has done in her own life. The series is rapidly expanding, highlighting women in cities from coast to coast, celebrating their contributions and inspiring others to follow their lead.

Leigh's expertise and passion for leadership and empowerment have made her a sought-after speaker, with multiple appearances on the TEDx stage. Her stories of kindness and personal growth have been featured in prominent publications like *HuffPost* and shared through appearances on *The Today Show* and the *Rachael Ray Show.*

As the founder of Kindleigh, a movement focused on giving back through acts of kindness, Leigh has led initiatives that have raised significant funds for charitable causes. Her mission is to create lasting change through kindness and sharing stories of impact, further solidifying her role as a leader in philanthropy.

Leigh resides in Southwest Florida with her son, Carter, and the love of her life. She's here to make an impact and leave her mark by illuminating others.

"Don't let the world change your heart. Let your heart change the world." - Leigh M. Clark

Instagram: @leighmclark @slaytheusa
www.leighmclark.com
www.slaytheusa.com

www.ingramcontent.com/pod-product-compliance
Lightning Source LLC
Chambersburg PA
CBHW061803120626
46550CB00005B/2109